John S. Pierson

Civil War in U.S.A.

John S. Pierson

Civil War in U.S.A.

ISBN/EAN: 9783742814135

Manufactured in Europe, USA, Canada, Australia, Japa

Cover: Foto ©Thomas Meinert / pixelio.de

Manufactured and distributed by brebook publishing software
(www.brebook.com)

John S. Pierson

Civil War in U.S.A.

NOTE.

A larger portion of the Songs in this collection
have been submitted to the editor by soldiers
in the Union Army, with the request that they
should be included in the Red, White, and Blue
Series, "as they are favorites in the camps." As
such they are here presented to the reader.

F. M.

New York, *April*, 1864.

CONTENTS.

viii CONTENTS.

CONTENTS. ix

CONTENTS.

LIST OF AUTHORS.

SONGS OF THE SOLDIERS.

—◆—

THE TWELFTH OF APRIL,

A. D. 1861.

BY EDMUND C. STEDMAN.

CAME the morning of that day,
    When the God, to whom we pray,
    Gave the soul of Henry Clay
        To the land ;
How we loved him — living, dying !
But his birthday banners flying,
Saw us asking and replying,
        Hand to hand.

For we knew that far away,
Round the fort in Charleston bay,
Hung the dark impending fray,
        Soon to fall ;

1

And that Sumter's brave defender,
Had the summons to surrender
Seventy loyal hearts and tender —
    That was all.

And we knew the April sun
Lit the length of many a gun —
Hosts of batteries to the one
    Island crag ;
Guns and mortars grimly frowning,
Johnson, Moultrie, Pinckney, crowning,
And ten thousand men disowning
    The old flag.

O, the fury of the fight
Even then was at its height !
Yet no breath, from noon till night,
    Reached us here ;
We had almost ceased to wonder,
And the day had faded under,
When — the echo of the thunder
    Filled each ear !

Then our hearts more fiercely beat,
As we crowded on the street,
Hot to gather and repeat
    All the tale ;

THE TWELFTH OF APRIL.

All the doubtful chances turning,
Till our souls with shame were burning,
As if twice our bitter yearning
    Could avail !

Who had fired the earliest gun ?
Was the fort by traitors won ?
Was there succor ?   What was done
    Who could know ?
And once more our thoughts would wander
To the gallant, lone commander,
On his battered ramparts, grander
    Than the foe.

Not too long the brave shall wait :
On their own heads be their fate,
Who against the hallowed State
    Dare begin ;
Flag defied, and compact riven !
In the record of high Heaven,
How shall Southern men be shriven
    For the sin ?

"SHOOT HIM ON THE SPOT."

A NATIONAL SONG.

BY WILLIAM ROSS WALLACE.

I.

WHEN Rebellion's impious hand
  Darkened o'er the loyal land,
Threatening its old flag unfurled,
Like a star-burst for the world —
Well our DIX, the firm-souled, cried,
From the mountain to the tide,
  " He who first that flag would lower,
    " SHOOT HIM ON THE SPOT!"

II.

Hark! — from yonder billow red,
Where devoted LAWRENCE bled;
From the hill where WARREN's blade
Freedom's sacred host arrayed;
From the tomb Potomac laves;
From ten thousand martyr-graves,
  Voices join that holy cry —
    " SHOOT HIM ON THE SPOT!"

III.

Hark ! — o'er Ocean answers swell !
Stirs the mountain-tomb of TELL !
Poland's lakes indignant roll,
Heaved by Koskiusko's soul !
Venice shakes her iron rack !
All, in chorus, thunder back —
    " *He who first that flag would lower,*
        " SHOOT HIM ON THE SPOT !"

IV.

Banner, given to our land
By a WASHINGTON's own hand,
Thou art floated o'er the sod
By the breath itself of God,
And the loyal spirit hears
That command from Heaven's spheres —
    "*He who first that flag would lower,*
        " SHOOT HIM ON THE SPOT !" *

  * See *New York Ledger*, April 5, 1862.

THE STARS AND STRIPES.

BY JAMES T. FIELDS.

RALLY round the flag, boys, —
　　Give it to the breeze!
That's the banner we love
　　On the land and seas.

Brave hearts are under it;
　　Let the *traitors* brag;
Gallant lads, fire away!
　　And fight for the flag.

Their flag is but a rag —
　　Ours is the *true* one;
Up with the Stars and Stripes!
　　Down with the new one!

Let our colors fly, boys —
　　Guard them day and night;
For victory is liberty,
　　And God will bless the right.

GOD BLESS OUR UNION.

BY JAS. M. STEWART.

HAIL to our Union ! our dear native land,
  Where Freedom, triumphant, her reign has
    begun ;
God bless our Union ! and long may it stand,
  The glorious Union! the many in one.
Proud of our birthright, we tell the glad story,
  While bearing thy banner bright over the sea;
Long, long may our children exult in thy glory,
  O Queen of the Nations! the fair and the free !

Hail to our Union! our dear native land,
  Where Freedom, triumphant, her reign has
    begun ;
God bless our Union ! and long may it stand,
  The glorious Union ! the many in one.
Foes shall not conquer nor traitors enslave thee,
  Nor sever the bond by our forefathers made ;
Thy God, who, united, from ruin will save thee,
  His presence thy shield, and His arm is thine aid.

Hail to our Union ! our dear native land,
  Where Freedom, triumphant, her reign has
    begun ;

God bless our Union ! and long may it stand,
  The glorious Union ! the many in one.
Hark ! where the clangor of battle is ringing,
  What sound rises high o'er the noise of the fight ?
'T is the war-cry of Freedom our heroes are sing-
      ing —
    " Strike ! brothers, for Union, for God, and the
      Right !

Hail to our Union ! our dear native 'land,
  Where Freedom, triumphant, her reign has
      begun ;
God bless our Union ! and long may it stand,
  The glorious Union ! the many in one.
Sing we, together, with joyous hosanna !
  Till nations remote shall unite in the song —
" The stars that now gleam in our glorious banner
  To God and to Freedom forever belong ! "

———◆———

UP AND AT THEM.

BY ALFRED B. STREET.

UP and at them
    Once again !
Freemen, up ! the way is plain,
At the traitors once again !

UP AND AT THEM.

Let not brief reverses daunt us;
  Let no craven fears assail;
Treason's banner now may taunt us
  In the fierce but fleeting gale;
But the time again will come,
  When again that flag shall cower
And the boasting voice be dumb,
  Shouting now its little hour!
    Up and at them!
Freemen, then, the way is plain!
At the traitors once again!

    Up and at them
      Once again!
Madmen! fiercely though ye drain
War's red chalice, it is vain!
Never shall ye rend asunder
  Freedom's flag of stripes and stars; —
Freedom guards it with her thunder;
  Down will smite your thing of bars;
Down your wretched counterfeit!
  In her roused and sacred rage,
She will tear and trample it!
  Holy is the war ye wage!
    Up and at them!
Freemen, then, the way is plain;
At the traitors once again!

Up and at them
Once again !
Though we bleed in every vein,
At the traitors once again !
By the nation's ancient story,
By the deeds of other days,
By our hopes of future glory
By the deep disdain or praise,
That our action now awaits,
As we yield or dare the strife ;
Let us, through all adverse fates,
Swear to guard the nation's life !
Up and at them !
Freemen, then, the way is plain ;
At the traitors once again !

—◆—

FREEMEN, TO YOUR STANDARD RALLY!

A Song of the Union Men of the South.

BY LEWIS J. CIST.

FREEMEN, to your standard rally !
Come from mountain, hill, and valley ;
Forth from town and city sally —
Swear to guard it and defend it ;

Round that flag, so long victorious,
Stars and Stripes, beloved and glorious,
Swear, with voice deep, not uproarious,
    This Rebellion foul to end it!

Shall the tree our fathers nourished —
Watered by their blood that flourished,
Till the haughty Briton perished
    Out the land — shall *it* be riven?
Shall the glorious flag they gave us—
Emblem high to guard and save us
'Gainst all foes that would enslave us —
    From our natal soil be driven?

Shall the UNION, which our sires
Forged in patriotic fires,
Perish at the fell desires
    Of the base secession crew?
Shall we let *such* knaves and traitors,
Robbers, thieves, and freedom-haters,
All our nation's great creators
    Most successful work undo?

No! by WASHINGTON and WAYNE,
ADAMS, FRANKLIN, LEE, and PENN,
All those brave, true-hearted men
    Who Freedom gained and Union gave us—

Up! and fight for Law and Order,
Fight until the last marauder
Ye have driven from your border,
   Who oppress and would enslave us!

By that bright and proud array —
Patriot names of later day —
JACKSON, WEBSTER, WIRT, and CLAY,
   Statesmen, orators, and sages, —
Who have battled, "armed men strong,"
For the Right against the Wrong,
That their country loved might long
   Stand the hope of unborn ages.

By the God of heaven above us,
By the dear ones loved, who love us,
By all motives pure that move us,
   The HERO's or the MARTYR's crown —
We will *never* yield us, never,
Till the fiends who seek to sever
Our loved country are forever
   And forevermore put down!

THE BATTLE SONG OF THE CHURCH.

FEAR not the foe, thou flock of God,
    Fear not the sword, the spear, the rod,
            Fear not the foe !
He fights in vain who fights with thee ;
Soon shalt thou see his armies flee,
            Himself laid low.

Come, cheer thee to the toil and fight ;
' T is God, thy God, defends the Right ;
            He leads thee on.
His sword shall scatter every foe,
His shield shall ward off every blow ; —
            The crown is won.

His is the battle, His the power,
His is the triumph in that hour ;
            In Him be strong.
So round thy brow the wreath shall twine,
So shall the victory be thine,
            And thine the song.

Not long the sigh, the toil, the sweat,
Not long the fight-day's wasting heat ;
            The shadows come.

Slack not thy weapon in the fight;
Courage ! for God defends the Right ;
    -     Strike home ! strike home !

———◆———

CAMP SONG.

BY CAPT. CHARLES WINTER

Written on receipt of the intelligence that the Massachusetts soldiers had been fired on in Baltimore.

AIR — " *Ye Parliaments of England.*"

WE tell you, Traitors of the South,
     With all your chivalry, too,
That madness whirls your brains about,
     And you know not what you do !
You have made a war, unholy ;
     You 'll be sure to rue the day
When you meet the Freemen of the North
     In battle's stern array !

You have called us dough-faced cowards,
     Said you'd meet us, two to one,
And you 've shown us how a dirty mob
     Can steal a soldier's gun ;

But for your dastard cowardice
  The battle-field shall tell
That the blood you shed in Baltimore
  Was your passport into hell !

You have dared us out to meet you,
  But you 'll find our courage true !
For, by the eternal God we swear
  To crush your Rebel crew !
We know our cause is holy;
  We will keep our powder dry ;
And fight, as did our noble sires,
  For Freedom — or we 'll die !

We march as loyal patriots !
  We are bound with iron bands !
Our trust is in a righteous God !
  Our swords are in our hands !
We march to conquer Treason ;
  Our purpose is our might,
And we do not fear the issue,
  For we know that WE ARE RIGHT.

We bear the glorious Stars and Stripes.
  That never knew defeat ;
We 'll drench with blood your Rebel rag
  And tread it 'neath our feet !

We 'll sweep this land from end to end ;
　We 'll burn from sea to sea ;
Till earth and heaven alike shall know
　AMERICA IS FREE !

And when at last we conquer,
　And the deadly strife is o'er,
The Stars and Stripes shall light the skies
　And float from shore to shore !
And from Oregon to Texas,
　And from Florida to Maine,
Shall Peace and Plenty crown the land,
　And Truth and Justice reign.

—◆—

BALTIMORE.

INSCRIBED TO THE MASSACHUSETTS SIXTH.

BY B. RUSH PLUMLY.

BLOOD of loyal Massachusetts,
　From the Rebel ground afar,
Loudly to the shaft of Bunker
　Cries the watchword of the war —
　　Cries it ever,
　　　　" Baltimore ! "

Till the granite breaks to speaking,
  Like the Theban shaft of old :
With its stony lips repeating
  To the Bay State, free and bold —
    Still repeating,
              " Baltimore ! "

Lo ! the merchant springs to battle
  From his Boston counting-room,
And the Lowell weaver rushes
  To the combat from the loom —
    To the combat,
              Baltimore !

From the mountain-men of Berkshire
  To the fishers of Cape Ann,
At old Bunker's Memnon-summons
  They are rising to a man —
    They are rising,
              Baltimore !

Rebel city ! thank thy true men
  That the Pilgrim sword and fire
O'er thy highways, red with murder,
  Still hath left a standing spire —
    Thank thy true men,
              Baltimore !

2

Onward! till the flag is flying
  O'er the cities of the South!
In the breath of Freedom breaking
  From the cannon's iron mouth —
    From the cannon,
          Baltimore!

———◆———

THE STARRY FLAG.

BY JOHN SAVAGE.

Air — "*Dixie's Land.*"

OH, the Starry Flag is the flag for me!
  'T is the flag of life! the flag of the free!
  Then hurrah, hurrah!
    For the Flag of the Union!
      Oh, the Starry Flag, &c.
We 'll raise that starry banner, boys,
  Hurrah! hurrah!
We 'll raise that starry banner, boys,
Where no power in wrath can face it!
  On town and field,
  The people's shield,

No treason can erase it !
   O'er all the land
   That flag must stand,
Where the people's might shall place it.

That flag was won through gloom and woe !
It has blessed the brave and awed the foe !
   Then hurrah ! hurrah !
     For the Flag of the Union.
      That flag was won, &c.
We 'll raise that starry banner, boys —
   Hurrah ! hurrah !
We 'll raise that starry banner, boys,
Where the Stripes no hand can sever !
   On fort and mast
   We 'll nail it fast,
To balk all base endeavor !
   O'er roof and spire,
   A living fire,
The Stars shall blaze forever

'T is the people's will, both great and small,
The rights of the States, the Union of all !
   Then hurrah, hurrah !
     For the Flag of the Union !
      'T is the people's will, &c.
We 'll raise that starry banner boys —

Hurrah! hurrah!
We'll raise that starry banner, boys —
Till it is the world's wonder!
    On fort and crag
    We'll plant that flag,
With the people's voice of thunder!
    We'll plant that flag,
    Where no hand can drag -
Its immortal folds asunder!

We must keep that flag where it e'er has stood,
In front of the free, the wise, and the good;
    Then hurrah! hurrah!
     For the Flag of the Union!
      We must keep that flag, &c.
We'll raise that starry banner, boys —
    Hurrah! hurrah!
We'll raise that starry banner, boys,
On field, fort, mast, and steeple!
    And fight and fall,
    At our country's call,
By the glorious flag of the people!
    In God, the just,
    We place our trust,
To defend the flag of the people.

SECESSION.

RESPECTFULLY DEDICATED TO GEN. BEAUREGARD.

THE sun's hot rays were falling fast,
  As through a Southern city passed
A man who bore, 'midst rowdies low,
A banner with the strange motto —
                    Secession !

His brow was sad ; his mouth beneath
Smelt strong of fire at every breath :
And like a furious madman sung
The accents of that unknown tongue —
                    Secession !

In happy homes he saw the light
Of household fires gleam warm and bright ;
Above, the spectral gallows shone,
And from his lips escaped a groan —
                    Secession !

" Try not that game ! " Abe Lincoln said,
" Dark lower the thunders overhead ;
The mighty North has been defied."
But still that drunken voice replied —
                    Secession !

"Oh! pause!" the Quaker said, "and think
Before thee leaps from off the brink!"
Contempt was in his drunken leer;
And still he answered, with a sneer —
       Secession!

"Beware the pine-tree's bristling branch!
Beware the Northern avalanche!"
And that was Scott's restraining voice;
But still this was the traitor's choice —
       Secession!

At close of war, as toward their homes
Our troops as victors hurried on,
And turned to God a thankful prayer,
A voice whined through the startled air —
       Secession!

A traitor by a soldier keen,
Suspended by the neck was seen,
Still grasping in his hand of ice
That banner, with this strange device —
       Secession!

There, to the mournful gibbet strung,
Lifeless and horrible he hung;

And from the sky there seemed to float
A voice like angel's warning note —
   Secession!

———◆———

COLUMBIA, QUEEN OF THE LAND AND THE SEA.

. BY GEORGE W. ELLIOTT.

A MERICA! Home of the free!
 To the stars of thy liberties bright
Turn the eyes of the millions who flee
 For the rescue from tyranny's night!
Though thy magical name and thy ensign unfurled
May enkindle some envy with joy in the world,
Yet the orbs of thy Union shall glow through all
  time,
While the nations of earth own their splendor sub-
  lime.

Chorus:

O, Columbia's banner, the flag of the free,
Shall be honored for aye, o'er the land and the sea!

Columbia's Queen of the land!
 For the heart of the nation, her throne,

She proclaims this benignant command,
    " Let the will of my people be known !
They are free from the scourge of oppression's fell
        rod;
They are free evermore in the worship of God !
And the ensign that beams o'er the land of my
        birth
Shall a welcome fling out for the bond of the
        earth !"

                    Chorus: .

O, Columbia's banner, the flag of the free,
Shall be honored for aye, o'er the land and the sea

    America !   Home of the free !
        'T is thy dear starry emblem that holds
    The enchantment that binds us to thee —
        All our fortune to thine — in its folds !
On the wretch who its lustre of glory would pall
Shall the furious vengeance of patriots fall;
Yes, thy flag shall be sacred wherever unfurled,
And shall awe every traitor and foe in the world !

                    Chorus :

O, Columbia's banner, the flag of the free,
Shall be honored for aye, o'er the land and the sea !

THE STARS AND STRIPES.

BY THOMAS WILLIAMS, OF ALLEGHANY, PENN.

AIR — " *Irish Jaunting Car.*"

BROTHERS of free descent were we, and native
    to the soil,
Knit soul to soul, in one great whole, fruit of our
    fathers' toil :
But when that bond of love was rent, the cry rose
    near and far,
To arms! to arms! long live the stripes! we know
    no " single star."
Chorus — Hurrah! hurrah! for the Union Flag,
        hurrah!
        Hurrah for the Union Flag, that knows
          no " single star."

So long as Southern arrogance forbore to touch that
    flag,
Full many a taunt we meekly bore, and many an
    idle brag :
But when on Sumter's battlements, the traitors did
    it mar,
We flung abroad that Union Flag, that ne'er shall
    lose a star.

Hurrah! hurrah! for the Union flag,
    hurrah!
Hurrah for the Union flag, that ne'er
    shall lose a star.

And first the gallant Keystone State, from every
    mountain-glen,
From hill and valley, lake and town, sent down her
    stalwart men ;
And all New England rose amain, as blew the trump
    of war,
And raised on high their fathers' flag that knows
    no single star.
        Hurrah! &c.

From Saratoga's tree-crown'd heights, from Mon-
    mouth's bloody plain,
The men of York and Jersey, too, both swelled the
    mustering train,
As onward — onward — fierce it rush'd o'er all
    opposing bars,
To punish those who dared insult our glorious Stripes
    and Stars.
        Hurrah! hurrah! for the Union flag,
            hurrah!
        Hurrah for the Union flag, with all its
            Stripes and Stars!

And next the hardy pioneers, the dauntless and the
    brave,
From those domains by Freedom won, that never
    knew a slave,
Their trusty rifles all in hand, with eye and port like
    Mars,
Grasped once again with iron hand, the staff that
    bears our stars!
        Hurrah! hurrah! for the Union flag,
           hurrah!
        Hurrah for the Union flag, that bears
           our Stripes and Stars!

And from the bison's prairie-haunts, o'er Mississip-
    pi's flood,
From Minnehaha's sparkling falls, from Kansas'
    land of blood,
New England's youngest scions there have heard
    the din of wars,
And grasped their fathers' ancient brand, and
    rear'd their stripes and stars,
And belted on their father's brand and rear'd
    their fathers' stars.
        Hurrah! &c.

And farther still, where sunset-seas bathe Califor-
    nia's shore,

And grim Sierras darkly frown its golden treasures
    o'er,
Our Western Twins have heard the call, and an-
    swer'd from afar,
We come! we come! Rear high the flag, that
    knows no single star.
        Hurrah! &c.

Missouri, too, her garments red, and little Dela-
    ware,
With heart as big as when of old she bore a lion's
    share,
Have burst the chain which cramps the soul, and all
    that 's noble mars,
And wheel'd in line, come weal or woe, beneath the
    Stripes and Stars.
        Hurrah! &c.

And "Maryland, *our* Maryland," though called with
    "fife and drum,"
And "old-line bugle," too, to fight against the
    "Northern scum,"
Has thought of Camden's bloody field and Eutaw's
    iron scars,
And lo! she stands, where erst she stood, beneath
    the Stripes and Stars.
        Hurrah! &c.

Would we could say the same of thee, thou dark
    and bloody ground !
Whose sexless sages, false of heart, a way of *peace*
    have found !
Shame on you ! No half faith would we ! Up,
    gird ye for the wars,
And take your place as *men* once more, beneath the
    Stripes and Stars.
        Hurrah ! &c.

From thy Medusa glance we turn, with hearts of
    cheer and pride,
To West Virginia, virgin rib, torn from false moth-
    er's side.
Daughter of strife ! Fair Freedom's child ! Thy
    mountains ring afar,
With echoing shouts for that best flag that counts
    another star.
        Hurrah ! &c.

And more 't will count, no Pleiad lost, of all that
    shining host,
Though dim eclipse have veil'd their fires, and trai-
    tors loudly boast ;
But one by one those wand'ring lights shall gem our
    heavens, like Mars,

And all the nations bless our stripes and coronet of
 stars !
   Hurrah ! &c.

No other flag shall ever float above our homes or
 graves,
Save yonder blazing *oriflamme*, that flutters o'er
 our braves ;
Its rainbow-stripes, our Northern lights — with no
 sinister bars ;
Our ancient flag ! our fathers' flag ; our glorious
 Stripes and Stars !
   Hurrah ! &c.

Then bear that banner proudly up, young war-
 riors of our land,
With hearts of love, and arms of faith, and more
 than iron hand !
Down with the Northern renegade ! and join our
 gallant tars,
In rearing high, in victory, our deathless Stripes and
 Stars !
   Hurrah ! &c.

THE CALL.

HARK! 't is the trumpet's peal!
Which is borne on the evening breeze.
With lingering step two lovers walk,
And the moon looks down through the tall oak-trees.

Hark! 't is the trumpet's peal!
It calls to die in Freedom's name.
On their winding way the lovers pause,
And the youth's eyes kindle and flash like flame.

Hark! 't is the trumpet's peal!
It rings aloud from hill to vale:
While heart pressed to heart the lovers stand,
And the maiden weeps as her cheek grows pale.

Hark! 't is the trumpet's peal!
It rises o'er the cannon's roar.
His sword gleams bright as he dashes on,
And the maiden is praying alone in her bower.

Hark! 't is the trumpet's peal!
A hero's death his country weeps;
And far away a maiden lies cold,
While the moon on high her silent watch keeps.

A. A. H.

WAR-SONG OF THE UNION.

BY JONAS B. PHILLIPS.

AIR — "*The Standard-Bearer.*"

TO arms, ye brave! obey your country's call,
    Which summons ye to honor and to glory;
Resolv'd and sworn to conquer or to fall
    Defending our proud flag, so famed in story.
Now traitors dare assail that banner bright,
    And seek our bond of Union to sever!
          Arise, ye Free!
          Our battle-cry shall be
The Union, and the Stars and Stripes forever!

To arms! arouse! behold the loyal North,
    From city, hill, and mountain, and from valley,
Now sends her sons in gallant cohorts forth,
    Who to their country's standard bravely rally.
No star shall be effac'd, no traitor hand
    The Gordian knot of Union shall sever!
          Arise, ye Free!
          Our battle-cry shall be
The Union, and the Stars and Stripes forever!

Disgrace and shame upon the traitors rest,
　Whose parricidal hands assail the nation ;
Their names accurs'd, their memories unblest,
　Remembered but with honest execration !
No treason e'er so base as theirs — shall wo
　Surrender or forgive ?   By Heaven, never !
　　　　Arise, ye Free !
　　　　Our battle-cry shall be
　The Union, and the Stars and Stripes forever !

March on ! march on ! no cause was e'er so just
　As that by which we now are call'd to duty ;
With hearts resolved, in God we place our trust,
　And soon in all its bright and pristine beauty
Again shall proudly wave that flag of light,
　Which unto foe has been surrendered never !
　　　　Arise, ye Free !
　　　　Our battle-cry shall be
　The Union, and the Stars and Stripes forever !

THE SWORD, FLAG, AND PLOUGH.

A<small>IR</small> — *"Red, White, and Blue."*

I.

UNSHEATHED is the sword of the nation !
  Baptized in the blood of the brave,
The blade shall be Freedom's salvation
  To break the last bond of the slave.
From river and mountain and valley,
  Goes upward the patriot's vow,
And the legions of Liberty rally,
  To follow the Sword, Flag, and Plough.
Chorus — To follow the Sword, Flag, and Plough,
      To follow the Sword, Flag, and Plough ;
      And the legions of Liberty rally
      To follow the Sword, Flag, and Plough !

II.

Unfurl the Free Banner wherever
  The dawnings of victory gleam,
And perish the traitor's endeavor
  To darken fair Liberty's dream !
The echoes of triumph are ringing
  Where heroes are conquering now,
And the valor of Freed-men is bringing
  Success to the Sword, Flag, and Plough !

Success to the Sword, Flag, and Plough,
Success to the Sword, Flag, and Plough;
And the valor of Freed-men is bringing
Success to the Sword, Flag, and Plough !

III.

The Sword is the last liberator
The Angel of Justice has sent,
And freemen were false to their nature
To rivet a chain that is rent !
The heart of a people rejoices,
The symbol of treason must bow,
And a chorus of jubilant voices —
Hurrah for the Sword, Flag, and Plough !
Hurrah for the Sword, Flag, and Plough !
Hurrah for the Sword, Flag, and Plough !
And a chorus of jubilant voices
Hurrah for the Sword, Flag, and Plough !

A. M. I.

THE ARMY OF THE FREE.

DIVISION SONG OF PORTER'S DIVISION, ARMY OF THE POTOMAC.

BY FRANK H. NORTON.

AIR — " *Benny Havens.*"

IN the army of the Union we are marching in
        the van,
And will do the work before us, if the bravest
        soldiers can ;
We will drive the Rebel forces from their strong-
        holds to the sea,
And will live and die together in the Army of the
        Free.
Chorus — The Army of the Free, the Army of the
        Free ;
                We will live and die together in the
                Army of the Free.

We may rust beneath inaction, we my sink beneath
        disease,
The summer sun may scorch us or the winter's
        blasts may freeze,

But whatever may befal us, we will let the Rebels
see,
That unconquered, we shall still remain the Army
of the Free.
  The Army of the Free, the Army of the
   Free;
  Unconquered, we shall still remain the
   Army of the Free.

We are the best Division of a half a million souls,
And only resting on our arms till the war-cry on-
ward rolls;
When our gallant General Porter calls, why ready
we shall be,
To follow him forever with the Army of the Free.
  The Army of the Free, the Army of the
   Free;
  We will follow him forever, with the Army
   of the Free.

We have Butterfield the daring, and we've Martin-
dale the cool,
Where could we learn the art of war within a bet-
ter school,
Add Morell to the list of names, and we must all
agree,
We have the finest Generals in the Army of the
Free.

> The Army of the Free, the Army of the
> Free ;
> We have the finest Generals in the Army
> of the Free.

Though we live in winter-quarters now, we 're waiting but the hour,
When Porter's brave Division shall go forth in all
its power,
And when on the field of battle, fighting we shall be,
We 'll show that we cannot disgrace the Army of
the Free.

> The Army of the Free, the Army of the
> Free ;
> We 'll show that we cannot disgrace the
> Army of the Free.

Then hurrah for our Division; may it soon be call'd
to go,
To add its strength to those who have advanced to
meet the foe ;
God bless it, for we know right well, wherever it
may be,   [Free.
'T will never fail to honor our great Army of the
> The Army of the Free, the Army of the
> Free,
> > 'T will never fail to honor our great Army
> > of the Free.

SONG OF THE IRISH LEGION.

BY JAMES DE MILLE.

E Pluribus Unum! Erin go Bragh!

YE boys of the sod, to Columbia true,
   Come up, lads, and fight for the Red, White,
   and Blue!
Two countries we love, and two mottoes we'll share,
And we'll join them in one on the banner we
     bear:
    Erin, mavourneen! Columbia, agra!
    E pluribus unum! Erin go bragh!

Upon them, my lads! and the Rebels shall know
How Erin can fight when she faces the foe;
If they can't give us arms, sure, we need n't delay;
With a sprig of shillalah we'll open the way.
     Erin, mavourneen! Columbia, agra!
     E pluribus unum! Erin go bragh!

"Blood-Tubs" and "Plug-Uglies," and others
     galore,
Are sick for a thrashing in sweet Baltimore;
Be Jabers! that same I'd be proud to inform
Of the terrible force of an Irishman's arm.

Erin, mavourneen !   Columbia, agra !
E pluribus unum !   Erin go bragh !

Before you the tyrant assembles his band,
And threatens to conquer this glorious land ;
But it wasn't for this that we traversed the sea,
And left the Green Isle for the land of the free.
Erin, mavourneen !   Columbia, agra !
E pluribus unum !   Erin go bragh !

Go forth to the tyrant, and give him to know
That an Irishman holds him his bitterest foe ;
And his sweetest delight is to meet him in fight,
To battle for freedom, with God for the right !
Erin, mavourneen !   Columbia, agra !
E pluribus unum!   Erin go bragh !

—◆—

PATRIOTIC SONG.

Tune — "*British Grenadiers.*"

UP, up, ye gallant freemen ;
    Hear, hear, the traitors call :
" We 'll plant our flag at Washington,
    Float it o'er Faneuil Hall ! "

"Never!" from out a million throats
  Leaps ready answer true;
Huzza, huzza, huzza, huzza!
  For the Stripes and Starry blue!

The sun, in rising, touches
  The shaft on Bunker Hill,
And on the Heights of Dorchester
  At eve lies calm and still;
And as of old, beneath their shades,
  Beat loyal hearts and true;
Huzza, huzza, huzza, huzza!
  For the Stripes and Starry blue!

Green lie the plains of Lexington,
  Watered with patriot-gore;
Sires of such sons as lately fell
  In traitorous Baltimore;
And hearts like theirs by thousands come,
  And Freedom's vow renew;
Huzza, huzza, huzza, huzza!
  For the Stripes and Starry blue!

Our faith and love and patience
  Have long been sorely tried;
" Let us alone," the haughty South
  With insolence have cried;

And while they cry, the murderous shot
  O'er gallant Sumter flew ;
Huzza, huzza, huzza, huzza !
  For the Stripes and Starry blue !

From city, farm, and workshop,
  Now countless legions pour,
To stand beneath the noble flag
  Raised by their sires of yore ;
Their country calls, they onward press,
  And still the shout renew ;
Huzza, huzza, huzza, huzza !
  For the Stripes and Starry blue !

ARMY-SONG.

DEDICATED TO THE FORTY-FOURTH REGIMENT.*

TUNE — " *Scots wha hae wi' Wallace bled.*"

FROM Katahdin's snowy crest,
  To Mount Vernon's sacred rest,
Through imperial valleys West,
           Shout the battle-cry.

* Massachusetts Volunteers.

Hark ! it is your conntry's call !
Lo ! she bids her brave sons all
Make the bands of traitors fall,
             In recreant graves to lie.

Would you see our broad domain,
By giant treason rent in twain,
In border-strifes your children slain ?
             Back as cowards fall.

Would you see our banner bright,
Wave untorn in Freedom's light,
Brave the world's united might ?
             Strike, then, once for all.

Come from homes you love so dear,
Come with hearts that know no fear,
Come with might in bow and spear,
             Down bid slavery go.

By the prayers our fathers breathed,
By the trusts to us bequeathed,
By the hopes our hearts which heaved,
             Smite oppression low.

Hail our UNION's new birthnight!
See it girt with grander might,
Ray out now a purer light,
    To the nations round.

 When our last victory is won,
 When the work of blood is done,
 And to our loved homes we come,
    To God shall praises sound.
         SELIM.

——◆——

THE ZOUAVES' BATTLE-SONG.

BY J. HOWARD WAINWRIGHT.

ONWARD, Zouaves, Ellsworth's spirit still leads
   us ;
Onward, Zouaves, for our country still needs us ;
Onward, Zouaves, for our banner floats o'er us ;
Onward, Zouaves, for the foe is before us ;
 Chorus — Onward, Zouaves,
   Do nothing by halves,
    Home to the hilt with the bay'net,
    Zouaves.

Onward, Zouaves, for the foe hath defied us ;
Onward, Zouaves, we have brave men to guide us ;
Let the sunlight and moonlight, from bayonets
    glancing,
Tell the foe the vanguard of the North is advancing.
        Onward, &c.

Onward, Zouaves, till we break down oppression ;
Onward, Zouaves, till we crush out secession ;
We 've shown them our friendship is honest and
    true,
We 'll show them our wrath can be terrible too.
        Onward, &c.

Onward, Zouaves, for our bugles are clanging ;
Onward, Zouaves, the assassins need hanging ;
No longer we 'll bear with their rapine and wrong,
Their guilt makes them weak while our cause
    makes us strong.
        Onward, &c.

Onward, Zouaves, — when the struggle is ended
Homeward we 'll carry the flag we 've defended ;
Home, where our dear ones will greet with caress-
    ings ;
Home where our country will greet us with bless-
    ings.
        Onward, &c.

Onward, Zouaves, till the traitors are punished;
Onward, Zouaves, till the treason hath vanished;
Onward, Zouaves, till once more in communion,
O'er the North and the South floats the flag of our
    Union.
    Onward, &c.

THE LITTLE DRUMMER.

A SOLDIER'S STORY.

BY R. H. STODDARD.

I.

'TIS of a little drummer,
   The story I shall tell;
Of how he marched to battle,
   And all that there befell.
Out in the West with Lyon,
   (For once the name was true,)
For whom the little drummer beat
   His *rat-tat-too*.

II.

Our army rose at midnight,
   Ten thousand men as one,

Each slinging on his knapsack,
  And snatching up his gun :
" *Forward!* " and off they started,
  As all good soldiers do,
When the little drummer beats for them
  The *rat-tat-too.*

III.

Across a rolling country,
  Where the mist began to rise ;
Past many a blackened farm-house,
  Till the sun was in the skies :
Then we met the Rebel pickets,
  Who skirmished and withdrew,
While the little drummer beat and beat
  The *rat-tat-too.*

IV.

Along the wooded hollows
  The line of battle ran,
Our centre poured a volley,
  And the fight at once began ;
For the Rebels answered shouting,
  And a shower of bullets flew ;
But still the little drummer beat
  His *rat-tat-too.*

v.

He stood among his comrades,
  As they quickly formed the line,
And when they raised their muskets
  He watched the barrels shine !
When the volley rang, he started !
  For war to him was new ;
But still the little drummer beat
  His *rat-tat-too.*

vi.

It was a sight to see them,
  That early autumn day,
Our soldiers in their blue coats,
  And the Rebel ranks in gray :
The smoke that rolled between them,
  The balls that whistled through,
And the little drummer as he beat
  His *rat-tat-too !*

vii.

His comrades dropped around him, —
  By fives and tens they fell,
Some pierced by Minnie bullets,
  Some torn by shot and shell ;
They played against our cannon,

And a caisson's splinters flew;
But still the little drummer beat
   His *rat-tat-too !*

VIII.

The right, the left, the centre —
   The fight was everywhere :
They pushed us here, — we wavered, —
   We drove and broke them there.
The gray-backs fixed their bayonets,
   And charged the coats of blue,
But still the little drummer beat
   His *rat-tat-too !*

IX.

" Where is our little drummer ? "
   His nearest comrades say,
When the dreadful fight is over,
 . And the smoke has cleared away.
As the Rebel corps was scattering
   He urged them to pursue,
So furiously he beat and beat
   The *rat-tat-too !*

X.

He stood no more among them,
   For a bullet as it sped
   4

Had glanced and struck his ankle,
   And stretched him with the dead !
He crawled behind a cannon,
   And pale and paler grew :
But still the little drummer beat
   His *rat-tat-too !*

XI.

They bore him to the surgeon,
   A busy man was he :
" A drummer boy — what ails him ? "
   His comrades answered, " See ! "
As they took him from the stretcher,
   A heavy breath he drew,
And his little fingers strove to beat
   The *rat-tat-too !*

XII.

The ball had spent its fury :
   " A scratch," the surgeon said,
As he wound the snowy bandage
   Which the lint was staining red !
" I must leave you now, old fellow. "
   " O take me back with you,
For I know the men are missing me,
   And the *rat-tat-too !* "

XIII.

Upon his comrade's shoulder
  They lifted him so grand,
With his dusty drum before him,
  And his drum-sticks in his hand !
To the fiery front of battle,
  That nearer, nearer drew, —
And evermore he beat, and beat,
  His *rat-tat-too !*

XIV.

The wounded as he passed them
  Looked up and gave a cheer:
And one in dying blessed him,
  Between a smile and tear !
And the gray-backs — they are flying
  Before the coats of blue,
For whom the little drummer beats
  His *rat-tat-too.*

XV.

When the west was red with sunset,
  The last pursuit was o'er ;
Brave Lyon rode the foremost,
  And looked the name he bore !
And before him on his saddle,

As a weary child would do,
Sat the little drummer fast asleep,
With his *rat-tat-too.*

FLAG-SONG OF THE MICHIGAN VOLUNTEERS.

BY D. BETHUNE DUFFIELD.

Adapted to the Anvil Chorus from Trovatore.

I.

TRUMPET, and ensign, and drum-beat are call-
        ing,
  From hill-side and valley, from mountain and
      river,
"Forward the flag!" e'en though heroes are falling,
  Our God will His own chosen standard deliver.

Chorus :

Star-Spangled Banner! our hopes to thee are
        clinging,
Lead us to victory, or wrap us in death —
To thee stanch are we, while yet a breath
Remains to sing thee ;
Or arm to fling thee,
O'er this fair land, wide and free.

II.

" Union and Freedom ! " our war-cry is rolling,
  Now over the prairie, now wide o'er the billow,
Hark 't is the battle, and soon will be tolling
  The knell of the soldier, who rests 'neath the
    willow.
        Star-Spangled Banner, &c.

III.

Banner triumphant ! though grand is thy story,
  We 'll stamp on thy folds, in this struggle to-day,
Deeds of our armies, transcending in glory
  The bravest yet chanted in Poesy's lay.
        Star-Spangled Banner, &c.

IV.

Wise were our fathers, and brave in the battle,
  But treason uprises their Union to sever,
Rouse for the fight ! shout aloud 'mid War's rattle,
  The Union must triumph, must triumph forever !
        Star-Spangled Banner, &c.

V.

Trumpet, and ensign, and drum-beat are calling,
  From hill-side and valley, from mountain and
    river,

" Forward the flag ! " e'en though heroes are falling,
Our God will His own chosen standard deliver.

Chorus :

Star-Spangled Banner ! our hopes to thee are
clinging,
Lead us to victory, or wrap us in death.

DETROIT, *April* 20, 1861.

SONG OF THE SOLDIER.

BY GEORGE W. PUTNAM.

TUNE — *" Shining Shore."*

THE moon has set — the signal light
    Sends high its solemn warning !
We sleep upon our arms to-night
    And wait the battle morning.

Chorus :

    We march beneath the Stripes and Stars,
        God's banner ! — let earth bless it !
    Yet to it every knee shall bow,
        And every tongue confess it !

Again the signal light gleams forth,
    And hark ! — the " long roll " beating !

To arms ! — fall into line and give
  The foe a freeman's greeting.
    We march, etc.

If we fall on the battle-field,
  Friends, let there be no sighing ;
There is in all the universe
  No better place for dying !
    We march, etc.

A few years more, a few years less,
  What matters it, my brother ?
Our duty done — we 'll fearless pass
  From this world to the other.
    We march, etc.

This thought shall sweeten life's last hour —
  Our Heavenly Father sees us ;
Die humbly for the human race,
  As once died holy Jesus.
    We march, etc.

But see ! red shot and hissing shell
  The Southern skies illuming !
And hark ! the Northern answer, in
  The cannon's sullen booming !
    We march, etc.

Hurrah ! the bugles sound the charge !
O sturdy Northern yeomen !
With tempest stride and serried steel,
Sweep down upon the foemen !
We march, etc.

The trampled of the distant lands
Watch, pray, and hope, and wonder !
The slaves shout in the barracoon,
As through the breach we thunder !
We march beneath the Stripes and Stars,
God's banner ! — let earth bless it !
Yet to it every knee shall bow,
And every tongue confess it !

———◆———

PENNSYLVANIA RANGERS' WAR-SONG.*

BY JAMES Y. MURRAY.

AIR—"*I'm Afloat.*"

MOUNT! mount! and away o'er our borders
so wide ;
The sabre's our sceptre, the fleet steed our pride !
Up ! up ! with our flag, let its bright *stars* gleam
out —

* Dedicated to Colonel E. G. Chormann.

Mount! mount! and away on the wild border-
    scout!
We care not for danger, we heed not the foe;
Where our brave steeds can bear us, right onward
    we go,
And never, as cowards, can we fly from the fight,
While our belts bear a blade, for our cause it is
    right.

Then mount and away! give the fleet steed the
    rein —
The Ranger's at home on the wide-spreading plain;
Spur! spur in the chase, dash on to the fight,
Cry vengeance for the North! and God-speed the
    right!
The might of the foe gathers thick on our way,
They hear our wild shout as we rush to the fray;
What to us is the fear of the death-stricken
    plain?
We have " braved it before and will brave it again."

The death-dealing bullets around us may fall —
They may strike, they may kill, but they cannot
    appall;
Through the red field of carnage right onward
    we'll wade,

While our guns carry ball and our hands wield the
blade.
Hurrah, my brave boys! we may fare as we please,
No *Southern* banner now floats in the breeze!
'T is the flag of Columbia that waves o'er each
height, —
The Stars and Stripes over all shed their light.

———◆———

HO! YANKEE BOYS THROUGHOUT THE WEST.

BY R. TOMPKINS.

HO! Yankee boys throughout the West,
Hear ye the traitor's shout,
" We'll build the Union up again,
And leave New England out! "
And shall we join the rabble-cry,
At tyranny's command?
Traduce the homes our childhood loved,
Betray our father-land?
Chorus — And shall we join the rabble-cry,
At tyranny's command?
Traduce the homes our childhood loved,
Betray our father-land?

Forget the days we rambled o'er
   Our free New England hills ?
Forget the joyous hours we passed,
   Beside her shining rills?
Forget the cheerful fires, whose smoke
   Upon her free air curls ?
Forget the hearths where cluster round
   New England's peerless girls ?
      Forget the cheerful, &c.

What I look with alien eyes upon
   The land where Hancock died,
And in a vile and impious tone
   The Pilgrim's faith deride ?
Shall Lexington and Bunker Hill
   Be named by us in scorn,
Because a Revolution there
   In Freedom's name was born ?
      Shall Lexington, &c.

No ! by the blood of heroes shed
   On Bunker's gory height ;
No ! by the mem'ry of the dead
   Who dared old England's might —
The flag that floats o'er Plymouth Rock
   Shall wave o'er Sumter's wall !

These States shall all together stand,
   Or all together fall !
     The flag, &c.

We 've met the boasting cavalier, —
   Proud lord of whips and chains, —
Within our nation's council-halls
   And conquered him with brains ;
And now, if he will have it so,
   We 'll make the Southron feel
The Pilgrims' sons, wherever found,
   Can handle lead and steel.
     And now, if he, &c.

The torch that burned at Lexington,
   Lit by our patriot sires,
Shall yet illume the Southern skies,
   With Freedom's holy fires ;
And Yankee schools shall dot the plains,
   And Yankee churches rise,
Till truth and light dissolves each chain
   And slavery groans and dies.
     And Yankee schools, &c.

BALTIMORE.

BY SETH BONNEY,

OF COMPANY C, MASSACHUSETTS SIXTH.

THE night is dark, the camp is stilled,
    Each soldier's heart with joy is thrilled;
He dreams of home and scenes gone past,
Not conscious but his dream can last.
    Chorus — Baltimore! Baltimore!
        He starts at the cry of Baltimore.

A mystic grandeur fills his breast,
While peaceful slumber brings him rest;
He little thinks of dangers near,
His dream unmixed with dread or fear.
    Baltimore! Baltimore! &c.

At length the guard with watchful eye
Discovers danger lurking nigh;
Reminded of the days before,
He gives the cry of " Baltimore! "
    Baltimore! Baltimore! &c

Quick the soldier's ready ear
Warns him of the foe that's near;

He springs out in the dreary night
From slumber, to defend the Right.
    Baltimore! Baltimore! &c.

Baltimore! The alarming word
Thrills the heart where'er 't is heard;
Suggests the loss of brothers gone,
Justice calls the foe to atone.
    Baltimore! Baltimore! &c.

When duty calls so loud and plain,
With sorrow he recalls the slain;
And as sacred is the brother's dust,
So sacred is this cause and just.
    Baltimore! Baltimore! &c.

As long as the free their blood shall give,
Our country shall so long survive;
And where the weak the strong implore,
The rallying cry shall be " Baltimore!"
    Baltimore! Baltimore! &c.

SONG OF THE ANDERSON ZOUAVES.

BY MISS EDDA MIDDLETON.

Tune — "*The Red, White, and Blue.*"

WHEN Sumter, the shrine of the nation,
 Was struck by black Treason's command,
And our flag, from its world-renowned station,
 Was dragged and defiled in the sand,
A shout that presaged desolation
 To the homes of the traitorous crew
Shook the earth to its firmest foundation —
 The shout for " the red, white, and blue."
Chorus — Three cheers for the Anderson Zouaves !
    Three cheers for the Anderson Zouaves !
    Our flag shall yet wave over Sumter,
    Placed there by the Anderson Zouaves.

And when our strong Temple was burned
 And battered by Treason's red hand,
Its flames to fierce lightnings were turned,
 Its smoke to black clouds o'er the land
The storm iron hailstones was spouting,
 As south on the north wind it flew ;
And iron-mouthed thunders were shouting,
 " All hail ! to the red, white, and blue."

Then Anderson, faithful forever,
  Called forward, to lead in the van,
Those who will dishonor him never,
  His Zouaves, his invincible clan.
Then strike for home, country, and glory —
  For loved ones we always strike true :
His name lives forever in story
  Who falls 'neath " the red, white, and blue."

The cup — not the wine-cup — bring hither,
  Salt tears fill it up to the brim ;
It is wreathed with no wreath that will wither —
  The prayers of our loved ne'er grow dim.
Thus pledge we our Patron and Heaven,
  As patriots, brave, pure, and true :
To our country shall Sumter be given,
  Or we fall 'neath " the red, white, and blue."
     Three cheers for the Anderson Zouaves !
     Three cheers for the Anderson Zouaves !
     Our flag shall yet wave over Sumter,
     Placed there by the Anderson Zouaves.

THE MASSACHUSETTS LINE.

BY ROBERT LOWELL.

AIR — " *Yankee Doodle.*"

I.

STILL first, as long and long ago,
   Let Massachusetts muster ;
Give her the post right next the foe ;
   Be sure that you may trust her.
She was the first to give her blood
   For Freedom and for Honor ;
She trod her soil to crimson mud :
   God's blessing be upon her !

II.

She never faltered-for the Right,
   Nor ever will hereafter ;
Fling up her name with all your might,
   Shake roof-tree and shake rafter.
But of old deeds she need not brag,
   How she broke sword and fetter ;
Fling out again the old striped flag !
   She 'll do yet more and better.

5

III.

In peace her sails fleck all the seas,
  Her mills shake every river ;
And where are scenes so fair as these
  God and her true hands give her ?
Her claim in war who seek to rob ?
  All others come in later —
Hers first it is to front the Mob,
  The Tyrant and the Traitor.

IV.

God bless, God bless the glorious State !
  Let her have way to battle !
She 'll go where batteries crash with fate,
  Or where thick rifles rattle.
Give her the Right, and let her try,
  And then, who can, may press her ;
She 'll go straight on, or she will die ;
  God bless her ! and God bless her !

DUANESBURGH, *May 7, 1861.*

WAR-SONG OF THE ESSEX CADETS.*

WHERE gallant Buxton leads the way,
  His company so true
Shall follow to the battle-field
  And shout their wild halloo.
    Halloo! halloo! halloo! my boys,
     For Buxton leads the way;
    Our hearts are free, and true is he,
    And we must win the day.

And Buxton, though in stature small,
  In heart is stout and brave;
We love him and we 'll follow him
  Till we meet a soldier's grave;
    Or till sweet victory shall crown
     Our banner of the free;
    Hurrah! hurrah! for Buxton then,
    Hurrah for victory.

Then come our brave Lieutenants, who
  Inspire us with true hope,
The second's valiant Taggard, and
  The first is noble Pope;

* Massachusetts Volunteers.

And D, our gallant company,
  May it with foeman cope.
Hurrah, my boys, for Buxton,
  For Taggard and for Pope.

Hurrah for our true company,
  The gallant boys of D,
Hurrah for gallant Volunteers,
  Wherever they may be.
    Halloo! halloo! halloo! my boys,
      For Union and for Right,
    And may the God of Armies guide
    Our Captain in the fight.

———◆———

SONG OF THE LYON REGIMENT.

BY J. G. FORMAN.

TUNE — *"Bruce's Address."*

ONWARD, now, ye true and brave!
  Heaven inspire our patriot-band!
We must now our country save,
  And guard our native land.

" Onward ! " then our watchword be !
  " Onward ! " still our rallying cry !
For our country's liberty
  We 'll conquer or we 'll die !

To her valiant sons she cries,
  Up, and arm you for the fight !
Meet the traitors as they rise,
  And put their hordes to flight !
Strike, to aid your country's cause,
  Strike ! for Liberty and Right !
Strike ! for Justice and the Laws,
  By your glorious might !

On the bloody field of Mars,
  Noble deeds must now be done ;
Bear aloft the Stripes and Stars,
  Until the field is won.
Onward, then, ye true and brave !
  Rear your glorious standard high,
Freedom's banner proudly wave
  In death or victory !

With the sword of Liberty,
  Strike foul Treason to the dust !
Let each foreign despot see
  That our cause is just.

Onward, then, ye true and brave!
  Heaven our country's hope defend!
He, whose arm is strong to save,
  Will keep us to the end.

Onward to the battle-field,
  Valiant Lyon led the brave;
He fell beneath his red-cross shield,
  And fills a hero's grave!
" Onward!" was his dying word;
  Hallowed may his memory be,
Who with valor drew his sword,
  And fought for Liberty!

Bear aloft his glorious name!
  On our standard rear it high!
We will guard his spotless fame,
  And bravely do or die!
Onward, then, ye true and brave!
  Your avenging swords unsheathe;
Freedom's banner proudly wave,
  In victory or death!

"ONLY NINE MILES TO THE JUNCTION."

WRITTEN BY H. MILLARD,

COMPANY A, SEVENTY-FIRST REGIMENT, N. Y. S. M.

TUNE — " *The other Side of Jordan.*"

THE troops of Rhode Island were posted along
  On the road from Annapolis-station,
As the Seventy-first Regiment, one thousand strong,
  Went on in defence of the nation.
We 'd been marching all day in the sun's scorching
    ray,
  With two biscuits each as a ration,
When we asked Gov. Sprague to show us the way,
  And " How many miles to the Junction ? "
Chorus — How many miles, how many miles,
      How many miles to the Junction ?
        When we asked Gov. Sprague to show us
         the way,
          And " How many miles to the Junc-
           tion ? "

The Rhode Island boys cheered us on out of sight,
  After giving the following injunction :
" Just keep up your courage — you 'll get there
    to-night,
  For 't is only nine miles to the Junction."

They gave us hot coffee, a grasp of the hand,
   Which cheered and refreshed our exhaustion,
We reached in six hours the long-promised land,
   For 't was " only nine miles to the Junction."
       Only nine miles, &c.

And now as we meet them on Washington's streets,
   They always do hail us with unction,
And still the old cry some one surely repeats,
   " 'T was only nine miles to the Junction ! "
Three cheers for the warm-hearted Rhode Island
     boys,
   May each one be true to his function,
And whene'er we meet, let us each other greet,
   With " only nine miles from the Junction."
       Only nine miles, &c.

Nine cheers for the flag under which we will fight,
   If the traitors should dare to assail it ;
One cheer for each mile we made on that night,
   When 't was " only nine miles to the Junction."
With hearts thus united — our breasts to the foe —
   Once again with delight we will hail it;
If duty should call us, still onward we 'll go,
   If even " nine miles to the Junction."
       Only nine miles, &c.

BAY-STATE SONG.

"They had sent word to us from Philadelphia that we could not pass through that city, (Baltimore,) but the Colonel made up his mind that we could; and so we did.
. . . You may depend upon it that wherever we are ordered, we shall do our duty, and not make a blot on the records of Massachusetts."

Letter from a Private of the Sixth Mass. Regiment.

"The cause of Baltimore is the cause of the whole South."
A. H. STEPHENS.

TUNE — "*There is Rest for the Weary.*"

'TIS the old Bay State a-coming,
  With the Pine-tree waving high,
Foremost where the fight is thickest,
  Freedom still her battle-cry.
From the rocky shore of Plymouth,
  From the plains of Lexington,
From beneath the shaft of Bunker,
  Every hero sends a son.
Chorus — To the fray comes the Bay State,
      Clear the way for the Bay State,
      Trust you may in the Bay State,
        She will do or die !

From our dear old Berkshire mountains,
  From Cape Cod's sea-beaten sand,

With one cry we rush to battle, —
    Freedom and our native land!
From the quiet graves of Concord,
    Still as in our fathers' day,
Where her country's need is greatest,
    Massachusetts leads the way.
        To the fray, &c.

Onward dash the Pine-tree banner,
    Where a threatened Senate calls,
Ere a foe in Freedom's city
    Desecrate her sacred halls.
Where a son would strike a mother,
    With a traitor's stealthy blow,
Forward! every loyal brother,
    Fly to crush the dastard foe.
        To the fray, &c.

Onward, then, our stainless banner,
    Let it kiss the Stripe and Star,
Till in weal and woe united,
    They forever wedded are.
We will plant them by the river,
    By the gulf and by the strand,
Till they float, to float forever,
    O'er a free, united land.
        To the fray, &c.

We have left the plough and anvil,
   Left the ledger and the loom ;
Our shares to swords are beaten,
   And our pen 's the pen of doom.
But we 'll plough a deeper furrow,
   And we 'll deal a heavier blow,
And upon the Nation's ledger
   We will strike the balance now.
      To the fray, &c.

Lay the rails and build the engines,
   O'er the stream the bridges throw ;
These are little Yankee notions,
   Yankees carry as they go.
To the friends we leave behind us
   Oft we pledge a hearty health, —
And one prayer to God we offer, —
   Save the good old Commonwealth !
      To the fray, &c.

See an Adams and an Otis
   Look from heaven to speed us on !
Hear a Warren and a Prescott
   Bid us keep the fields they won !
See again Virginia's Patriot
   Rise to bid Disunion stand !

See the shade of Monticello
　　Strike again at Treason's hand!
　　　To the fray, &c.

Forward, then, the Pine-tree banner!
　　Still, as in our fathers' day,
Where her country's need is greatest,
　　Massachusetts leads the way!
By our brothers' blood still crying
　　From the streets of Baltimore,
Let the foe who struck behind them,
　　Be struck down forevermore.
　　　To the fray, &c.

Now, the Stars and Stripes forever
　　Be he cursed, each traitor-son,
Who assails the starry banner,
　　And the flag of Washington!
For Mount Vernon's sacred ashes
　　Will not rest within their bed,
With a traitor-band around it,
　　And a traitor-flag o'erhead.
　　　　To the fray comes the Bay State,
　　　　Clear the way for the Bay State,
　　　　Trust you may in the Bay State;
　　　　　She will do or die!

THE SEVENTY-NINTH.*

BY THOMAS FRAZER.

AIR — "*Here 's to the Year that 's awa'.*"

COME, muster, my bonny brave Scots,
    An' muster your clans one an' a',
Nor heed who else lags, so the free thistle wags,
    When Treason drives Right to the wa';
For Freedom, for Union, an' Law,
    We 'll do a' that true men may dare;
An' come weal or come scaithe, for these to the
      death —
    The Seventy-ninth will be there !

Come, stir, then, an' trim for the work ;
    Come, Borderer, Lowlander, Celt,
An' wi' firelock in hand our tartan-clad band
    Will soon mak the auld grit be felt.
We 'll show how auld Scotland for truth
    Has bluid in her heart yet to spare,
An' let us but ken when the truth may want
      men —
    The Seventy-ninth will be there !

* New York State Militia.

Then heeze out the pipes wi' a cheer,
 An' up wi' some heart-thrillin' strain,
To mind us the field is where Scots never yield,
 While ae chance to win may remain.
Syne shout, lads, the auld battle-cry —
 " Saint Andrew ! " — an' let them beware
When doure Southron knaves wad mak North-folk
   their slaves —
 The Seventy-ninth will be there !

The Union, the Nation, an' Name,
 The " Stars and the Stripes " an' the Laws !
Oh ! never can hand wave the death-dealing brand
 In what could be holier cause !
Then muster, my bonny brave Scots,
 An' swear by the tartan we wear,
Where e'er be the van, one in heart to a man —
 The Seventy-ninth will be there !

A GATHERING SONG.

Tune — " The Campbells are Coming."

A VOICE from the East and a voice from the
West,
A voice from the shade where the patriots rest,
A voice from the vales, and each echoing height,
On the ear it breaks through the dropped curtain
of night;
The voice of a trumpet, it pealeth afar,
And thrills through the nation a trumpet of war;
From the roar of the lakes to the ocean's wide
bound,
A marshalling host doth reëcho the sound.

Chorus:
They gather! they gather! true-hearted and brave!
While star-spangled banners exultingly wave;
He who sits on the stars with His sceptre of might
Sustaineth the arm which supporteth the Right.

The cattle are grazing beneath the green shade,
The ploughshare is left in the unfurrowed glade,
The counting-house merchant, from day-book and
dues,
Is lost in the current of martial reviews;

The veteran warrior doth buckle once more,
The falchion which flashed through the battle of
        yore,
With sons and with grandsons, yes ! *all* for the foe,
To raise the old standard, the Rebel lay low.
    They gather, they gather, &c.

Then haste to the rescue, ye patriot sons,
Your birthright to prove, as the favorite ones ;
Strike, manfully strike, till your country shall be
Entirely redeemed as the home of the free.
Yet Bunker Hill's State, as of old in its zeal,
The foremost responds to our nation's appeal,
While first upon Liberty's altar to mourn
The sons of her pride, by foul treachery torn.
    They gather, they gather, &c.

They 've roused the old lion, Scott, out of his lair,
No claw lined with cotton, for Dixie, is there !
He 'll chase that fox, Davis, in front of his host, ·
And send him, with Haman to wander, twin-ghost ;
While President Lincoln is valiant and bold,
To deal with opposers, like Abra'am of old ;
His sword upon tyrants the patriarch drew,
Redeeming his kinsman — *our* Abra'am will, too !
    They gather, they gather, &c.

Our country is calling; wake, sons of the true!
The storm of Fort Sumter was thundered at *you;*
Each shell that whizzed there, and each traitorous
    gun,
Was aimed at the banners your fathers have won.
    Then gather, then gather, &c.

Yet pause in your songs, let the banners float low,
Half-mast o'er the turf, while a nation's tears flow!
As young Zouaves in the soil which he loved make
    a grave
For their golden-souled leader, — young Ellsworth
    the brave.
When bearing the olive of freedom and peace,
Our Eagle, returning, bids slaughter to cease,
Shall History place on the charter of fame,
First in death, first in glory, that young martyr's
    name.

BIVOUAC-SONG OF THE FIFTY-THIRD REGIMENT.*

AIR — "*Auld Lang Syne.*"

WHILE black Disunion rears its head
  In this — fair Freedom's land,
So long we 'll sing a warlike strain,
  And be a warlike band.
Our flag 's unfurled — the Stars and Stripes
  We ever will maintain ;
The traitor dies who boldly dares
  That glorious flag to stain,
Chorus — We 're resting now in bivouac,
      And one day's march is made,
    We 'll sing a song while twilight sinks
      Into the night's deep shade.

Our brave young leader cheers us on,
  Our officers are true,
We trust in them, they trust in us —
  Whate'er they say we do.
We know we 'll never die of thirst,
  While our gallant BROOKE is full ;

* Pennsylvania Volunteers.

And when our rations all are gone,
  We 'll still have left a BULL.
    We 're resting now in bivouac, &c.

When Rebel balls fly thick and fast,
  As if to learn us "dots,"
We 'll make them feel our sharp sword's steel,
  And fight behind our POTTS.
For old BEAU — we have no — REGARD,
  He 'll soon be in the lurch,
And go below, as all do know,
  While we trust in our CHURCH.
    We 're resting now in bivouac, &c.

Then let us sing a happy song
  Around our camp-fire bright,
Of friends at home — the girls we love —
  We 'll dream of them to-night;
Yes, as we rest upon the ground,
  Beside our trusty gun,
We 'll dream of loved ones far away —
  Of battles fought and won.
    We 're resting now in bivouac, &c.

THE SEVENTH.*

BY FITZJAMES O'BRIEN.

Air — "*Gilla Machree.*"

I.

OCH! we 're the boys
    That hearts desthroys
Wid making love and fighting;
    We take a fort,
    The girls we court,
But most the last delight in.
    To fire a gun,
    Or raise some fun,
To us is no endeavor;
    So let us hear
    One hearty cheer —
The Seventh's lads forever!
Chorus —For we 're the boys
    That hearts desthroys,
Wid making love and fighting;
    We take a fort,
        The girls we court,
        But most the last delight in.

* New York State Militia, Colonel Lefferts.

THE SEVENTH.

II.

There 's handsome Joe,
Whose constant flow
Of merriment unfailing,
Upon the tramp,
Or in the camp,
Will keep our hearts from ailing.
And B—— and Chat.,
Who might have sat
For Pythias and Damon,
Och! whin they get
Their heavy wet,
They get as high as Haman.
For we 're the boys
That hearts desthroys, &c.

III.

Like Jove above,
We 're fond of love,
But fonder still of victuals;
Wid turtle-steaks
An' codfish cakes
We always fills our kittles.
To dhrown aich dish,
We dhrinks like fish,
And mum 's the word we ulther;

An' thin we swill
Our Léoville,
That oils our throats like butther.
For we 're the boys
That hearts desthroys, &c.

IV.

We make from hay
A splindid tay,
From beans a gorgeous coffee;
Our crame is prime,
Wid chalk and lime —
In fact, 't is quite a throphy.
Our chickens roast,
Wid butthered toast,
I 'm sure would timpt St. Pether;
Now you 'll declare
Our bill of fare
It could n't be complether.
For we 're the boys
That hearts desthroys, &c.

V.

Now silence all,
While I recall
A memory sweet and tender;

The maids and wives
That light our lives
With deep, enduring splendor —
We 'll give no cheer
For those so dear,
But in our hearts we 'll bless them,
And pray to-night,
That angels bright
May watch them and caress them.
For we 're the boys
That hearts destroys,
Wid making love and fighting;
We take a fort,
The girls we court,
But most the last delight in.

———◆———

SONG FOR THE ILLINOIS VOLUNTEERS.

BY "AGNES."

WE are *nobles* of the Prairie, and we come, and
we come,
To fight for Law and Liberty, and our dear prairie-
home ;
No craven hearts, or coward hands, are numbered
in our ranks,

Our souls were never shackled with the chains that
    Slavery clanks.
      We are free, we are free,
      And we ever mean to be,
      For ever, ever free,
      In death or victory !

Our banner is a galaxy of glorious silver stars,
Freedom's history is written on its white and crimson
    bars,
In the face of Southern foes we will flaunt our dear
    old flag,
And it never shall be lowered to a vile Secession
    rag :
      It shall wave forever free,
      For ever, ever free,
      Or a winding-sheet shall be,
      For us and Liberty.

Our Southern foes are brothers — Oh God ! and
    must we strike
At bosoms born and nurs'd with us, on Freedom's
    soil alike ?
Alas ! unblushing treachery has stamped the South-
    ern name,
With deeds so dark they mark anew the calendar
    of shame.

We will teach them that to be
Truly, loyally free,
Is the surest guarantee
Of precious liberty.

When the bugles loudly blow, and the booming
     guns declare
That the fiery torch of battle is lighted by their
     glare,
With hearts unchilled by fear, in trust that God is
     near,
We will show our Rebel foes we fight for all we
     hold most dear.
          They shall see, they shall see,
          Although no " chivalry,"
          We can die for Liberty —
          Death, death, or Liberty !

THE IRISH-AMERICAN'S SONG.

BY SCHUYLER CONWAY.

AIR — "*Robin Adair.*"

WOULD we desert you now,
           Flag of the Free ;
When we a solemn vow,
           Flag of the Free,
You from all harm to save,
Made when we crossed the wave,
And you a welcome gave,
           Flag of the Free ?

Whose aid to cheer us came,
           Flag of the Free,
When to proud England's shame,
           Flag of the Free,
Famine swept o'er our land ;
Death ravaged ev'ry band,
And loosed the tyrant's hand,
           Flag of the Free ?

Are we now cowards grown,
           Flag of the Free ?
Would we you now disown,
           Flag of the Free ?

You to whose folds we fled ;
You in whose cause we 've bled,
Bearing you at our head,
                    Flag of the Free ?

Could we desert you now,
                    Flag of the Free,
And to black traitors bow,
                    Flag of the Free ?
Never ! through good and ill
Ireland her blood will spill,
Bearing you onward still,
                    Flag of the Free !

———◆———

SONG OF THE ANDERSON CAVALRY.

BY GEORGE H. BOKER.

THERE were tears in the eyes we left behind,
    And sighs on the lips we kissed at starting ;
Nor blush we to find our sight half blind,
    As we think again of that bitter parting.
Chorus — For we go, we go, with parry and blow,
            And harder we 'll fight as our numbers
            grow few ;

To fight for the only banner we know —
  The Stripes and the Stars on the field
    of blue.

Oh! for the love of the hearts in grief and fear,
  Our swords flashed out from the scabbards
    that bound them;
And more surely here do we guard our dear,
  Than close by their sides with our arms around
    them.
        For we go, we go, &c.

Let cowards prate what they'll do at needs,
  When steel's at the breasts of our helpless wo-
    men;
We saddle our steeds, and whatever our deeds,
  We'll show to the eyes of our Rebel foemen.
        For we go, we go, &c.

Then onward, my boys, with a ringing cheer,
  With cracking carbine and glittering sabre;
Let the pale foe hear from vanguard to rear,
  How our troopers welcome their noble labor.
        For we go, we go, &c.

SOLDIERS' SONG.

BY ALICE CARY.

SING, brother soldiers,
  Sing near and far,
For the light of hope is breaking
  From the red flower of war;
Breaking, and brightening
  Amazingly grand,
On the black battle-smoke
  That drives through the land.

Sing, brother soldiers,
  Sing near and far,
For the light of peace is breaking
  From the red flower of war.
The light of peace is breaking,
  And all men agree
We are bound to have a country,
  Where every soul is free !

Sing, brother soldiers,
  Sing near and far,
For the light of love is breaking
  From the red flower of war.

The light of love is breaking
From the red and reeking sod,
And man is new-created
In the image of his God.

SKEDADDLE.

BY T. B. ALDRICH.

THE shades of night were falling fast,
As through a Southern village passed
A chap who bore, not over-nice
A banner with the odd device,
Skedaddle !

His hair was red; his toes beneath
Peeped, like an acorn from its sheath,
While with a frightened voice he sung
A burden strange to Yankee tongue,
Skedaddle !

He saw no household fire, where he
Might warm his tod or hominy :
Beyond the Cordilleras shone,
And from his lips escaped a groan,
Skedaddle !

" O, stay,"'' a cullered pusson said,
" An' on dis bosom res' your hed !"
The Octoroon she winked her eye,
But still he answered, with a sigh,
  Skedaddle !

" Beware McCLELLAN, BUELL, and BANKS,
Beware of HALLECK's deadly ranks !"
This was the planter's last good-night ;
The chap replied, far out of sight,
  Skedaddle !

At break of day, as several boys
From Maine, New York, and Illinois,
Were moving southward, in the air
They heard these accents of despair,
  Skedaddle !

A chap was found, and at his side
A bottle, showing how he died,
Still grasping in his hand of ice,
That banner with the odd device,
  Skedaddle !

There in the twilight, thick and gray,
Considerably played out he lay ;
And through the vapor, gray and thick,
A voice fell, like a rocket-stick,
  Skedaddle !

THERE LET HIM SWEETLY SLEEP.＊

BY GEORGE W. BUNGAY.

I.

"TENDERLY touch him," gently raise
The fallen hero ; let his praise
Sound sweetly through the future days,
    For he was brave and true.
Lean him against a manly breast,
Close to the heart that loves him best,
Like a tired traveller taking rest,
    Under the arch of blue.

II.

Then bear him to the sylvan shade,
Where dew falls from the drooping blade,
Like tears from the sad-hearted maid,
    Whose grief no words unfold.
Where the soft wind in sorrow sighs,
Among wild-flowers, whose pleasant eyes
Repeat the beauty of the skies, —
    Starlight and blue and gold.

III.

Brush from his brow the wind-tossed hair,
Mingled like cloud and sunshine there,

＊ Written in relation to the death of General Lyon.

Kiss the cold cheek, so pale and fair,
    In silent sorrow weep.
Fold his bronzed hands upon his breast,
And when the day fades in the west,
Under the green turf let him rest,
    In calm, unbroken sleep.

IV.

Hollow his grave where the green sod,
By traitor's feet has ne'er been trod,
Where sweet flowers are the smile of God,
    For the patriot, pure and true.
There let a graceful, fadeless tree,
Emblem of hope and liberty,
Arise; his epitaph shall be
    Sweet flowers, red, white, and blue.

V.

Bury him where the brook shall sing
His requiem, and returning spring
Shall come with bloom and rustling wing,
    Each season from her throne;
And Heaven shall watch with starry eyes,
That sleep not in the stooping skies,
The tomb to which an angel flies
    To roll away the stone.

7

SOLDIER'S SONG.

BY JOHN G. NICOLAY.

THE wide world is the soldier's home,
  His comrades are his kin;
His palace-roof the welkin dome,
  The drum his mandolin.
    He gives to air
    All thoughts of care,
  And trolls his serenade
    To fiery Mars,
    The king of stars,
  That never love betrayed.

The banner is the soldier's bride,
  The love of bold and brave;
His wedding-feast, the battle-tide;
  His marriage-bed the grave.
    Where the bullets sing,
    Death's leaden wing,
  Light as a dancing feather,
    When hero falls,
    To glory's halls,
  Wafts life and love together.

ON BOARD THE CUMBERLAND.

MARCH 7, 1862.

BY GEORGE H. BOKER.

STAND to your guns, men !" Morris cried.
  Small need to pass the word ;
Our men at quarters ranged themselves,
  Before the drum was heard.

And then began the sailors' jests :
  " What thing is that, I say ? "
" A long-shore meeting-house adrift
  Is standing down the bay ! "

A frown came over Morris' face ;
  The strange, dark craft he knew ;
" That is the iron Merrimac,
  Manned by a Rebel crew.

" So shot your guns, and point them straight ;
  Before this day goes by,
We 'll try of what her metal 's made."
  A cheer was our reply.

" Remember, boys, this flag of ours
  Has seldom left its place ;

And where it falls, the deck it strikes
  Is covered with disgrace.

" I ask but this : or sink or swim,
  Or live or nobly die,
My last sight upon earth may be
  To see that ensign fly ! "

Meanwhile the shapeless iron mass
  Came moving o'er the wave,
As gloomy as a passing hearse,
  As silent as the grave.

Her ports were closed ; from stem to stern
  No sign of life appeared.
We wondered, questioned, strained our eyes,
  Joked — everything but feared.

She reached our range.   Our broadside rang,
  Our heavy pivots roared ;
And shot and shell, a fire of hell,
  Against her sides we poured.

God's mercy ! from her sloping roof
  The iron tempest glanced,
As hail bounds from a cottage-thatch,
  And round her leaped and danced ;

Or when against her dusky hull
   We struck a fair, full blow,
The mighty, solid iron globes
   Were crumbled up like snow.

On, on, with fast increasing speed,
   The silent monster came ;
Though all our starboard battery
   Was one long line of flame.

She heeded not, no gun she fired,
   Straight on our bow she bore ;
Through riving plank and crashing frame
   Her furious way she tore.

Alas ! our beautiful keen bow,
   That in the fiercest blast
So gently folded back the seas,
   They hardly felt we passed !

Alas ! alas ! my Cumberland,
   That ne'er knew grief before,
To be so gored, to feel so deep
   The tusk of that sea-boar !

Once more she backward drew a space,
   Once more our side she rent ;

Then, in the wantonness of hate,
  Her broadside through us sent.

The dead and dying round us lay,
  But our foemen lay abeam;
Her open port-holes maddened us;
  We fired with shout and scream.

We felt our vessel settling fast,
  We knew our time was brief,
"The pumps, the pumps!" But they who
    pumped,
  And fought not, wept with grief.

"Oh! keep us but an hour afloat!
  Oh! give us only time
To be the instruments of Heaven
  Against the traitors' crime!"

From captain down to powder-boy,
  No hand was idle then;
Two soldiers, but by chance aboard,
  Fought on like sailor-men.

And when a gun's crew lost a hand,
  Some bold marine stepped out,
And jerked his braided jacket off,
  And hauled the gun about.

Our forward magazine was drowned ;
 And up from the sick bay
Crawled out the wounded, red with blood,
 And round us gasping lay.

Yes, cheering, calling us by name,
 Struggling with failing breath,
To keep their shipmates at the post
 Where glory strove with death.

With decks afloat, and powder gone,
 The last broadside we gave
From the guns' heated iron-lips
 Burst out beneath the wave.

So sponges, rammers, and handspikes —
 As men-of-war's-men should —
We placed within their proper racks,
 And at our quarters stood.

" Up to the spar-deck ! save yourselves ! "
 Cried Selfridge. " Up, my men !
God grant that some of us may live
 To fight yon ship again ! "

We turned — we did not like to go ;
 Yet staying seemed but vain,

Knee-deep in water; so we left;
  Some swore, some groaned with pain.

We reached the deck.   There Randall stood:
  " Another turn, men — so! "
Calmly he aimed his pivot-gun :
  " Now, Tenny, let her go ! "

It did our sore hearts good to hear
  The song our pivot sang,
As rushing on from wave to wave
  The whirring bomb-shell sprang.

Brave Randall leaped upon the gun,
  And waved his cap in sport;
" Well done ! well aimed ! I saw that.shell
  Go through an open port."

It was our last, our deadliest shot;
  The deck was overflown ;
The poor ship staggered, lurched to port,
  And gave a living groan.

Down, down, as headlong through the waves
  Our gallant vessel rushed,
A thousand gurgling, watery sounds
  Around my senses gushed.

Then I remember little more ;
　One look to heaven I gave,
Where, like an angel's wing, I saw
　Our spotless ensign wave.

I tried to cheer.　I cannot say
　Whether I swam or sank ;
A blue mist closed around my eyes,
　And everything was blank.

When I awoke, a soldier-lad,
　All dripping from the sea,
With two great tears upon his cheeks,
　Was bending over me.

I tried to speak.　He understood
　The wish I could not speak.
He turned me.　There, thank God ! the flag
　Still fluttered at the peak !

And there, while thread shall hang to thread,
　Oh ! let that ensign fly !
The noblest constellation set
　Against our northern sky.

A sign that we who live may claim
　The peerage of the brave ;

A monument, that needs no scroll,
  For those beneath the wave!

———◆———

BANNER-SONG, FOR APRIL, 1861.

BY EMELINE SHERMAN SMITH.

WHO said that the stars on our banner were
      dim —
That their glory had faded away?
Look up, and behold, how bright through each
    fold,
They are flashing and smiling to-day!
A few wandering meteors only, have paled —
  They shot from their places on high;
But the *fixed* and the *true* still illumine the blue,
  And will, while old ages go by.

Who said the fair temple, so patiently reared
  By heroes, at Liberty's call,
Was built insecure — that it could not endure,
  And was tottering e'en now to its fall?
False, false, every word! for that fane is upheld
  By the stoutest of hearts and of hands;
Some columns unsound may have gone to the
    ground,
  But proudly the temple yet stands.

Who said there were murmurs of grief in our midst,
    When loved ones departed to-day ?
Ah, no ! 't was not so ; every heart hushed its woe,
    And gave them " God-speed " on their way.
With their banner above, loving glances around,
    And blessings and prayers as a shield,
We trusted this band,— the fair flower of the land —
    To the perilous risks of the field.

Who said the good name of our country was gone,
    That her flag would be honored no more ?
Over valley and plain, over mountain and main,
    Rolls an answer like thunder's deep roar.
A million brave spirits all shout, with one voice,
    " We will die for the rights we demand !
Let traitors beware ! by their dark plots we swear,
    That no shadow shall rest on our land ! "

Who questions the promise ? Not we who behold
    This love, and this national pride,
Sweeping on through the clime, in a torrent
        sublime,
    And bearing all hearts on its tide.
Who fears for the issue ? Ah ! that must be left
    To the Mightiest Leader of all ;
While He holds the scale, Truth and Right must
        prevail,
    And Error and Treachery fall.

Then up with our banner! its stars never shone
  With a lustre so pure and so warm ;
Like a beacon's calm ray, pointing out the safe way,
  They gleam through this gathering storm.
This heart-cheering light led our fathers aright,
  Through all the dark perils they knew ;
The same magic glow shall lead us to the foe,
  And light us to *victory* too !

———◆———

PARTING HYMN.

BY OLIVER WENDELL HOLMES.

AIR — " *Dundee.*"

FATHER of Mercies, Heavenly Friend,
  We seek Thy gracious throne ;
To Thee our faltering prayers ascend,
  Our fainting hearts are known !

From blasts that chill, from suns that smite,
  From every plague that harms ;
In camp and march, in siege and fight,
  Protect our men-at-arms !

Though from our darkened lives they take
    What makes our life most dear,
We yield them for their country's sake
    With no relenting tear.

Our blood their flowing veins will shed,
    Their wounds our breasts will share ;
Oh, save us from the woes we dread,
    Or grant us strength to bear !

Let each unhallowed cause, that brings
    The stern destroyer, cease,
Thy flaming angel fold his wings,
    And seraphs whisper Peace !

Thine are the sceptre and the sword,
    Stretch forth Thy mighty hand —
Reign Thou our kingless nation's Lord,
    Rule Thou our throneless land !

THE ORDER OF THE DAY.

BY G. FORRESTER BARSTOW.

AIR— "*Jeannette and Jeannot.*"

THE morning light is breaking, the darkness
    disappears;
Away with idle sorrow, away with idler fears!
We are marching to the South, where we 'll find or
    force a way,
For Onward! Right Onward! is the Order of the
    Day.
Our country's flag is o'er us, and can traitors stand
    before us,
While the Stars and Stripes are gleaming in sum-
    mer's golden ray ?
No! we 'll bear that banner proudly, where the can-
    non thunders loudly,
We 'll bear it on in triumph through the thickest of
    the fray.

The bugle's note is sounding the summons to the
    fight,
A gallant leader guides us, and God defends the
    right;

We go to fight for Freedom, for the Union, for the
    Laws,
And never gallant soldiers fought for any nobler
    cause,
With the Stars and Stripes above us, with the
    prayers of those that love us,
All ready, all steady, we 're marching on our way :
The foe will fly before us, and Victory hover o'er
    us,
For Onward! Right Onward ! is the Order of the
    Day.

The call to arms has sounded on broad Atlantic's
    shore,
We catch its echo from the land that gleams with
    golden ore ;
From every Northern mountain, from every West-
    ern plain,
We come to clear our country's flag from every blot
    and stain.
The laurels that have crowned it, the wreaths that
    hang around it,
Won by our noble fathers on many a battle-plain,
No traitors' hand shall sever, but we 'll battle now
    and ever,
Till we bring the olden glory to the good old flag
    again.

THE YANKEE VOLUNTEERS.

*As sung by Private Ephraim Peabody, on the night after
the march through Baltimore.*

COME, all ye true Americans that love the
    Stripes and Stars,
For which your gallant countrymen go marching
    to the wars;
For grand old Massachusetts raise up three rousing
    cheers —
Three times three and a tiger for the Yankee
    Volunteers!

The nineteenth day of April they marched unto the
    war,
And on that day, upon the way, they stopped at
    Baltimore,
And trustingly expected the customary cheers
Which every loyal city gives the Yankee Volun-
    teers.
But suddenly in fury there came a mighty crowd,
Led on by negro-drivers, with curses long and
    loud;

With frenzied imprecations, with savage threats
  and sneers,
They welcomed to the city the Yankee Volunteers.

So furious grew the multitude, they rushed at them
  amain,
And a great storm of missiles came pouring like a
  rain.
Amid a thunderous clamor, such as mortal seldom
  hears,
They tried to cross the city, did the Yankee Volunteers.

The murderous storm of missiles laid many a soldier
  low,
Yet still these gallant hearts forbore to give the
  answering blow,
Till all the miscreants shouted, " They 're nearly
  dead with fears ;
We 'll hurry up and finish these Yankee Volunteers."

But, lo ! the guns are levelled, and loud the volleys
  roar,
And, inch by inch, they fight their way through the
  streets of Baltimore !

8

Before them shrunk the traitors, above them rise
    the cheers,
As through the throng, a myriad strong, march on
    the Volunteers.

Hurrah, then, for the old Bay State, that stood so
    well at bay !
Hurrah, for those who shed their blood, and gave
    their lives away !
For grand old Massachusetts, boys, let 's give three
    rousing cheers ! —
Three times three and a tiger for the Yankee
    Volunteers !

———◆———

RALLYING SONG OF THE SIXTEENTH REGIMENT IOWA VOLUNTEERS.*

Air — "*The Old Granite State.*"

WE have come from the prairies —
    We have come from the prairies —
We have come from the prairies
    Of the young Hawkeye State ;

---

* This song was written by a volunteer in the Sixteenth Regiment. He was a member of Captain Newcomb's company, and went from Dubuque.—*Dubuque Times.*

With our fathers' deeds before us,
And their starry banner o'er us,
For the land they rescued for us,
   We will welcome any fate.

We have left our cheerful quarters,
By the Mississippi's waters,
And our wives, and sons, and daughters,
   For the fierce and bloody fight;
But they will not deplore us,
With the foe encamped before us,
For the God who watches o'er us,
   Will himself protect the right.
Chorus — We have come from the prairies, &c..

From the dear Dubuque we rally,
And the swift Missouri's valley,
And to combat forth we sally,
   With the armies of the free;
Like the flood that flows forever,
We will flee the battle never,
But the waters of our river,
   We will follow to the sea.
      We have come from the prairies, &c.

Where our country's voice is calling,
Where the foeman's strokes are falling,

RALLYING SONG.

And the tide of war is rolling,
　To the far and sunny South;
Where our iron boats are speeding,
And our dauntless columns treading,
With the Mississippi leading,
　We are marching for its mouth.
　　　　We have come from the prairies, &c.

And whene'er our country needs us,
And where'er our banner leads us,
Never heeding what impedes us,
　We will follow to the death;
For the patriot must not falter,
When his country's foes assault her,
And profane her sacred altar,　　.
　With their pestilential breath.
　　　　We have come from the prairies, &c.

May our flag float on forever,
O'er a Union none can sever,
And may vile secession never
　Spread its ruin through our land;
May our country's wrongs be righted,
And her children reunited,
And her flag no more be blighted
　By the touch of Treason's hand.
　　　　We have come from the prairies, &c.

GOD FOR OUR NATIVE LAND.

BY REV. G. W. BETHUNE, D. D.

GOD'S blessing be upon
   Our own, our native land !
The land our fathers won
   By the strong heart and hand,
   The keen axe and the brand,
When they felled the forest's pride,
And the tyrant foe defied,
The free, the rich, the wide :
   GOD FOR OUR NATIVE LAND !

Up with the starry sign,
   The red stripes and the white !
Where'er its glories shine,
   In peace, or in the fight,
   We own its high command ;
For the flag our fathers gave,
O'er our children's heads shall wave,
And their children's children's grave !
   GOD FOR OUR NATIVE LAND !

Who doth that flag defy,
   We challenge as our foe ;
Who will not for it die,

Out from us he must go!
So let them understand.
Who that dear flag disclaim,
Which won their fathers' fame,
We brand with endless shame!
GOD FOR OUR NATIVE LAND!

Our native land! to thee,
   In one united vow,
To keep thee strong and free,
   And glorious as now —
   We pledge each heart and hand ;
By the blood our fathers shed,
By the ashes of our dead,
By the sacred soil we tread!
   GOD FOR OUR NATIVE LAND!

———◆———

IT IS GREAT FOR OUR COUNTRY TO DIE.

BY JAMES G. PERCIVAL.

OH! it is great for our country to die, where
   ranks are contending;
Bright is the wreath of our fame; glory awaits
   us for aye —

Glory that never is dim, shining on with light never
    ending —
  Glory that never shall fade, never, O never,
    away !

Oh! it is sweet for our country to die! How
    softly reposes
  Warrior youth on his bier, wet by the tears of
    his love,
Wet by a mother's warm tears; they crown him
    with garlands of roses,
  Weep, and then joyously turn, bright where he
    triumphs above.

Not to the shades shall the youth descend who for
    country hath perished;
  Hebe awaits him in heaven, welcomes him there
    with her smile;
There at the banquet divine, the patriot-spirit is
    cherished;
  God loves the young who ascend pure from the
    funeral pile.

Not to Elysian fields, by the still, oblivious river;
  Not to the isles of the blest, over the blue, rolling
    sea;

But on Olympian heights shall dwell the devoted
    forever;
  There shall assemble the good, there the wise,
    valiant, and free.

Oh! then how great for our country to die — in the
    front rank to perish,
  Firm, with our breast to the foe, Victory's shout
    in our ear!
Long they our statues shall crown, in songs our
    memory cherish;
  We shall look forth from our heaven, pleased the
    sweet music to hear.

THROUGH BALTIMORE.

THE VOICE OF THE PENNSYLVANIA VOLUNTEERS.

BY BAYARD TAYLOR.

I.

'TWAS Friday morn, the train drew near
  The city and the shore:
Far through the sunshine, soft and clear,
We saw the dear old flag appear,
And in our hearts arose a cheer
         For Baltimore.

II.

Across the broad Patapsco's wave,
  Old Fort McHenry bore
The starry banner of the brave,
As when our fathers went to save,
Or in the trenches find a grave,
                    At Baltimore.

III.

Before us, pillared in the sky,
  We saw the statue soar
Of Washington, serene and high —
Could traitors view that form, nor fly ?
Could patriots see, nor gladly die
                    For Baltimore ?

IV.

" Oh, city of our country's song,
  By that swift aid we bore
When sorely pressed, receive the throng,
Who go to shield our flag from wrong,
And give us welcome, warm and strong,
                    In Baltimore ! "

V.

We had no arms ; as friends we came,
  As brothers evermore,

To rally round one sacred name,
The charter of our power and fame :
We never dreamed of guilt and shame
                    In Baltimore.

VI.

The coward mob upon us fell :
  McHenry's flag they tore :
Surprised, borne backward by the swell,
Beat down with mad, inhuman yell,
Before us yawned a traitorous hell
                    In Baltimore !

VII.

The streets our soldier-fathers trod
  Blushed with their children's gore ;
We saw the craven rulers nod,
And dip in blood the civic rod —
Shall such things be, O righteous God,
                    In Baltimore ?

VIII.

No, never ! By that outrage black,
  A solemn oath we swore,
To bring the Keystone's thousands back,
Strike down the dastards who attack,
And leave a red and fiery track
                    Through Baltimore !

IX.

Dow down, in haste, thy guilty head !
God's wrath is swift and sore :
The sky with gathering bolts is red —
Cleanse from thy skirts the slaughter shed,
Or make thyself an ashen bed —
              Oh Baltimore !

IOWA MARCHING–SONG.

DEDICATED TO THE OFFICERS AND MEN OF THE THIRTY-EIGHTH
REGIMENT IOWA VOLUNTEERS.

BY SAMUEL M°NUTT.

AIR—" *Marseillaise.*"

WE come, we come from the land of prairie,
    Iowa, home of our hearts, afar ;
The flag of patriot sires we carry,
  The flag they loved in peace and war;
  The flag they loved in peace and war,
No traitor hand shall tear asunder
  This glorious flag, our fathers' pride —
  Nor shall the North and South divide,
By Rebel steel, or cannon thunder.
      Hurrah ! hurrah ! ye brave,
        Ye fearless Hawkeye band,
      March on, march on, march on to save
        Our Union and our land.

Hark, hark! the roar of war's commotion,
  Far over Southern hill and plain,
Thrills us, fills us with emotion,
  For friends beloved, and brothers slain —
  But our true flag we shall maintain.
Then welcome, boys, the field of battle;
  Let step be firm and eye be clear —
  God and the right — we feel no fear,
When bombs and balls around us rattle!
      Hurrah! hurrah! ye brave,
        Ye fearless Hawkeye band,
      March on, march on, march on to save
        Our Union and our land.

But this wild war is not our seeking,
  Oh, no, we ne'er began the strife,
Till traitor hands with blood were reeking,
  And aimed the murderer's red knife
  At Freedom, and the nation's life.
Let Southrons, now, but cease disunion,
  Cease now their worst of wicked wars,
  And join again the Stripes and Stars,
And North and South shall bloom in union.
      Hurrah! hurrah! ye brave,
        Ye fearless Hawkeye band,
      March on, march on, march on to save
        Our Union and our land.

THE MASSACHUSETTS JOHN BROWN SONG.

"The day of vengeance is in mine heart, and the year of my redeemed is come."—*Isaiah* lxiii.

OLD John Brown's body is a-mouldering in the
    dust,
Old John Brown's rifle's red with blood-spots
    turned to rust,
Old John Brown's pike has made its last, unflinch-
    ing thrust,
        His soul is marching on!
    Glory! Glory! Hallelujah!
     "Forward!" calls the Lord, our Captain:
    Glory! Glory! Hallelujah!
    With him we're marching on.

For treason hung because he struck at treason's
    root,
When soon palmetto-tree had ripened treason's
    fruit,
His dust, disquieted, stirred at Sumter's last salute —
        His soul is marching on!

Who rides before the army of martyrs to the word?
The heavens grow bright as He makes bare his
    flaming sword,
The glory fills the earth of the coming of the Lord —
        His soul is marching on!

" Thou soul the altar under, white-robed by mar-
   tyrdom !
Thy cry, ' How long, O Lord?' no longer finds me
   dumb ;
' Come forth !' calls Christ, ' the year of my redeemed is come ' —
            His soul is marching on·!

"And ye on earth, my army! tread down God's
   grapes till blood
Unto your horses' bridles hath out His wine-press
   flowed !
The day of vengeance dawns, — the day of wrath
   of God " —
            His soul is marching on !

His sacrifice we slay ! our sword shall victory crown !
For God and country strike the fiend Rebellion
   down !
For Freedom and the Right remember Old John
   Brown !
            His soul is marching on !
      " Glory ! Glory ! Hallelujah ! "
        Sings that army in the skies ;
      " Glory to the Lord, our Captain !"
        His army here replies.
Glory rings through heaven's arches,

Earth takes on the grand accord ;
" Glory ! " on to glory marches
The army of the Lord.

L. R.

———◆——

WAR-SONG.

BY T. P. ROSSITER.

COME, rally round our altar ;
No true heart now will falter,
When battles for our•freedom are to be fought
and won ;
Come, father, son, and brother ;
Leave sister, wife, and mother ;
There's work for strong arms doing, nor peace
until 't is done.
Chorus — For equal right
We only fight,
But while we breathe we will be free.
When our dear land
Our lives demands,
Die shouting, " God and Liberty ! "

List, how the drums are beating,
Their echoing tones repeating,

Come, rally! ho! come, rally, our hearths and
      homes to save;
    The blood our good sires left us,
    Though all else were bereft us,
Is heritage sufficient to keep from coward's grave.

    Come, flock around our standard,
    Come, crowd into the vanguard,
The beacons blazing brightly upon the hill-sides
    show
    There's need of arms united,
    With hearts for daring plighted,
To grapple in the death-grip which hellward hurls
    a foe.

    On our unguarded borders
    Throng hordes of fell marauders;
And our old flag, base miscreants insultingly would
    seize.
    Still Stars and Stripes are streaming,
    Thank God, in glory gleaming,
And patriot thrills are stirring as it flutters in the
    breeze.

    Our country now would prove us,
    While floats our flag above us,
Undaunted we'll give battle, nor drop the blade or
    brand,

Till all in place and station
Are loyal to the nation ;
Till enemies and traitors are driven from the land.

Leave shuttle, quit the harrow,
Bring from the mines strong marrow —
Leave anvil, plane, and compass, as the tocsin
sounds alarm ;
Leave mills and shops untended,
Leave books with tasks unended,
That wives and weans may nestle securely from all
harm.

Come, old, from the desk and study ;
Come, youth, with brawn arms ruddy ;
Come, rally ! ho ! come, rally for each altar, home,
and hearth ;
Our vows to each, now plighting,
In life and death uniting,
For Union we inherited, — God-given at our birth.

BANNER-SONG OF THE INDIANA ELEVENTH.

BY MRS. S. E. WALLACE.

AIR — "*Flag of our Union.*"

A SONG for our flag,
    A song for our band,
A song for the brave and the free !
    The motto we wear,
    United we stand,
Tried and true comrades are we.
    United in heart,
    United in hand,
A Union that time cannot sever ;
Chorus — A shout for our flag,
        A shout for our band,
Honor and Freedom forever.

    Unfurl the old flag,
    Let it float far on high ;
The chorus exulting ascend ;
    While one star remains
    We conquer or die,
By the banner we dare to defend.
    No cowardly heart,
    No traitorous hand,
Mars the Union that Time cannot sever ;
    · A shout for our flag, &c.

Where'er it may wave,
Our own standard-sheet,
By mountain, or river, or sea,
We press on the march
With unwearied feet,
While the gleam of its starlight we see.
Here 's to our friends,
A health and a hand,
Remembrance that time cannot sever;
A shout for our flag, &c

We 're all for the North,
For the South, too, we are,
United, unchanged, evermore;
No Palmetto flag
For us — no lone star,
But the Stripes and the old thirty-four.
Keep step to the song,
Be it right, be it wrong,
No State can the Union dissever;
Hurrah for the Stripes'
Hurrah for the Stars!
The Union, the Union forever!

VOLUNTEER CHORUS.

BY H. B. CORNWELL.

COME, sing to the praise of the good old days
    Of our brave grandsires before us,
Who bore to the wars our flag of stars,
    With a good old rousing chorus!
Through thick and thin, 'mid the battle's din,
    King George's rage defying,
They marched to the field, and would not yield,
    But kept the old flag flying!
Chorus — Then here 's three cheers for the Volun-
            teers !
        With traitors no communion !
        For the flag of the brave shall ever wave,
            For Liberty and Union !

To the sound of the drum, they come, come, come,
    From every hill and valley ;
Like the waves of the sea, for the Land of the
            Free
    With hearts of fire they rally !
On ! on ! to the fight, through the day, through the
            night ;
        There 'll soon be stormy weather !

By the girls we love we 'll heroes prove,
 And stand or fall together !
  Then here 's three cheers, &c.

Here 's the Green Mountain men from the wood
  and glen,
 And from each craggy highland,
And the Jersey Blue, with his rifle true,
 And the boys of stout Rhode Island !
The Empire State, who cannot wait,
 Crowds on from her furthest regions,
And the mighty West, from her teeming breast,
 Pours down her conquering legions !
  Then here 's three cheers, &c.

We 'll hang Jeff. Davis on a tree,
 Upon his own plantation !
And his reward give Beauregard,
 And charge it to the nation !
And we 'll bring from the wars the Stripes and
  Stars,
 When all our toils are over,
With a song to the praise of the good old days,
 And live and die in clover.
  Then here 's three cheers, &c.

UNION BATTLE-HYMN.

Air — "*Adeste Fideles*," or "*Portuguese Hymn.*"

'MID the battle's horror,
    That fills our land with sorrow,
We humbly raise our voices unto thee, Oh! Lord ;
.   *Chorus* — God of Creation,
           Helper of our nation,
           What Thou hast joined, oh! never
           Let human treason sever,
           But be our Guide forever, —
           Our Lord and King !

Now is the hour
That tries a Nation's power,
And seals the future fate of millions yet unborn.
        God of Creation, &c.

Has treason bereft us
Of what our fathers left us,
And shall we tamely bow unto the traitor's rule ?
        God of Creation, &c.

By the blood that bought us —
The faith our fathers taught us —
We 'll guard our sacred banner while a star remains !
        God of Creation, &c.

Souls of heroes o'er us
Are joining in our chorus,
As onward we are marching unto triumph or death !
God of Creation, &c.

Of our faults convict us,
For our sins afflict us,
But spare our blessed *Union*, oh ! Lord, we implore.
God of Creation,
Helper of our Nation,
. What Thou hast joined, oh ! never
Let human treason sever,
But be our Guide forever —
Our Lord and King !

———◆———

SONG OF THE MICHIGAN THIRD.

DEDICATED TO MISS KATE M'GINLEY.

FROM our peaceful homes in the far Northwest
We hastened long ago,
To rescue the Union's starry flag
From the clutch of the traitor-foe ;
And the tramp of our marching column
A hopeful promise gave,
Ere Sumter's echoes ceased to ring
O'er Michigan's startled wave.

And we 'll fight for the flag of our Union ;
    We 'll fight for our flag for aye,
Though every stripe be dyed in blood,
    And the last star shot away !

Through the frosts and storms of winter,
    'Neath the fiery summer sun,
We 've marched, and fought, and suffered,
    Nor yet is our toiling done ;
On half a score of bloody fields
    Our less'ning ranks have bled,
Where " Fighting Dick " won deathless fame,
    Or immortal Kearny led.
        Yet we 'll fight for our glorious banner,
            We 'll fight for our flag for aye,
        Though every stripe be dyed in blood,
            And the last star shot away !

A third of our gallant fellows
    Are resting from their toil,
And sleep the peaceful sleep of death,
    In " Virginia's sacred soil ";
" At home again," as many more,
    By disease and battle maimed,
Nurse mangled limbs and shattered health
    With spirits yet untamed.

Yet we 'll fight for the starry banner,
 We 'll fight for our flag for aye,
Though every stripe be dyed in blood,
 And the last star shot away !

Our numbers are few, our banner in shreds,
 But our hopeful hearts are strong,
And we 'll die as our noble mates have died,
 Ere Right shall succumb to Wrong ;
Aristocrats may recreant prove,
 And sacred trusts betray —
But Freedom's Temple shall not fall,
 By the " Mudsills " giving way.
  And we 'll fight for the flag of Freedom,
   We 'll fight for our flag for aye,
  Though every stripe be dyed in blood,
   And the last star shot away !
CAMP PITCHER, Va., *March*, 1863.

CAVALRY-SONG.

BY ELBRIDGE JEFFERSON CUTLER.

THE squadron is forming, the war-bugles play ;
 To saddle, brave comrades, stout hearts for a
  fray !
Our captain is mounted — strike spurs, and away !

No breeze shakes the blossoms or tosses the grain ;
But the wind of our speed floats the galloper's
        mane,
As he feels the bold rider's firm hand on the rein.

Lo ! dim in the starlight, their white tents appear !
Ride softly ! ride slowly ! the onset is near !
More slowly ! more softly ! the sentry may hear !

Now, fall on the Rebel — a tempest of flame !
Strike down the false banner whose triumph were
        shame !
Strike, strike for the true flag, for Freedom, and
        Fame !

Hurrah ! sheathe your swords ! the carnage is done.
All red with our valor, we welcome the sun.
Up, up with the stars ! we have won ! we have
        won !

BATTLE-SONG OF THE FIFTY-FIRST.

The following is the Battle-Song of the Fifty-first Regiment of New York, sung by them as they approached the coast of North Carolina.

SAY, Rebels, will you meet us,
 Say, Rebels, will you greet us,
Say, Rebels, will you beat us,
  On North Carolina shore ?
In the name of God we 'll meet you,
With the sword of God we 'll greet you,
By the grace of God we 'll beat you,
  On North Carolina shore ;
   Singing glory, hallelujah,
   Singing glory, hallelujah,
   Singing glory, hallelujah,
    To God for evermore !

With the sword of " Jeff." you meet us,
In the name of " Jeff." you greet us,
In Treason's cause to beat us,
  On North Carolina shore :
But our flag shall float forever,
And our Union none shall sever,
And treason punish ever,
  On North Carolina shore.

Oh ! then, glory, hallelujah,
Oh ! then, glory, hallelujah,
Oh ! then, glory, hallelujah,
To God for evermore !

------◆------

BRAVE BOYS ARE THEY.

HEAVILY falls the rain,
 Wild are the breezes to-night ;
But 'neath the roof, the hours as they fly
 Are happy, and calm, and bright.
Gathering round our fireside,
 Though it be summer-time,
We sit and talk of brothers abroad,
 Forgetting the midnight chime.
Chorus — Brave boys are they !
  Gone at their country's call ;
  And yet, and yet we cannot forget
  That many brave boys must fall.

Under the homestead roof
 Nestled so cosey and warm,
While soldiers sleep, with little or nought
 To shelter them from the storm,

Resting on grassy couches,
  Pillowed on hillocks damp;
Of martial fare, how little we know,
  Till brothers are in the camp.

Thinking no less of them,
  Loving our country the more,
We sent them forth to fight for the flag
  Their fathers before them bore.
Though the great tear-drops started,
  This was our parting trust:
God bless you, boys! we 'll welcome you home,
  When Rebels are in the dust.

May the bright wings of love
  Guard them wherever they roam;
The time has come when brothers must fight,
  And sisters must pray at home.
Oh! the dread field of battle!
  Soon to be strown with graves!
If brothers fall, then bury them where
  Our banner in triumph waves.
      Brave boys are they!
      Gone at their country's call;
      And yet, and yet we cannot forget
      That many brave boys must fall.

SONG OF THE THIRTEENTH REGIMENT, MAS-SACHUSETTS RIFLES.

DEDICATED TO LIEUTENANT JUDSON, COMPANY C.

WE go where cannon rattle on the road,
   We go where batteries frown !
And we riflemen feel as we cap and load,
  That the Rebel flag must come down !
         Come down,
    That the Rebel flag must come down !

We go where traitors battle against law ;
   We go with a vengeful shout !
And we soldiers know, as we enter the war,
  'T is for country we rush to their rout !
         Their rout,
    For our country we rush to the rout !

We come, with rifles levelled for a charge,
  And Rebels must fall before us !
But hearts of the Thirteenth Regiment are large,
  And give quarter where foes implore us !
         Implore us,
    When defeated foes implore us.

We come, with resolve mettled high in breast,
  The Stars and Stripes to sustain !
And our Eagle flies with us,* from sea-girt nest,
  The nation's life to maintain !
      To maintain,
  The nation's true life to maintain.

                                       B.

FREMONT'S BATTLE-HYMN.

BY JAMES G. CLARK.

OH, spirits of Washington, Warren, and Wayne !
  Oh, shades of the heroes and patriots slain !
Come down from your mountains of emerald and
    gold,
And smile on the banner ye cherished of old ;
Descend in your glorified ranks to the strife,
Like legions sent forth from the armies of life ;
Let us feel your deep presence, as waves feel the
    breeze,
When the white fleets, like snowflakes, are drank
    by the seas.

* On the banner presented at Fort Independence.

As the red lightnings run on the black, jagged
    cloud,
Ere the thunder-king speaks from his wind-woven
    shroud,
So gleams the bright steel along valley and shore,
Ere the combat shall startle the land with its roar.
As the veil, which conceals the clear starlight, is
    riven,
When clouds strike together, by warring winds
    driven,
So the blood of the race must be offered like
    rain,
Ere the stars of our country are ransomed again.

Proud sons of the soil where the Palmetto grows,
Once patriots and brothers, now traitors and
    foes,
Ye have turned from the path which our fore-
    fathers tród,
And stolen from man the best gift of his God;
Ye have trampled the tendrils of love in the
    ground,
Ye have scoffed at the law which the Nazarene
    found,
Till the great wheel of Justice seemed blocked for
    a time,
And the eyes of humanity blinded with crime.

The hounds of oppression were howling the knell
Of martyrs and prophets, at gibbet and cell;
While Mercy despaired of the blossoming years,
When *her* harp-strings no more should be rusted
    with tears.
But God never ceases to strike for the Right;
And the ring of His anvil came down through the
    night,
Though the world was asleep, and the nations
    seemed dead,
And Truth into bondage by Error was led.

Will the banners of morn at your bidding be
    furled,
When the day-king arises to quicken the world?
Can ye cool the fierce fires of his heat-throbbing
    breast,
Or turn him aside from his goal in the West?
Ah! sons of the plains where the orange-tree
    blooms,
Ye may come to our pine-covered mountains for
    tombs;
But the light ye would smother was kindled by One
Who gave to the universe planet and sun.

Go, strangle the throat of Niagara's wrath,
Till he utters no sound on his torrent-cut path;

10

Go, bind his green sinews of rock-wearing waves,
Till he begs at your feet like your own fettered
    slaves.
Go, cover his pulses with sods of the ground,
Till he hides from your sight like a hare from the
    hound ;
Then swarm to our borders and silence the notes
That thunder of Freedom from millions of throats.

———◆———

SONG OF THE SIXTY-NINTH.*

AIR—" *The Flag of our Union Forever.*"

THEN fling out the banner, on high let it wave
   O'er the land of the exile's affection,
And cursed be the coward, and branded the slave,
   Who refuses that flag his protection.

'T is the emblem of Freedom on sea and on land,
   No tyrant shall ever profane it ;
By Heaven, it shall thus continue to stand,
   Though we spill our heart's blood to maintain it.

* New York State Militia.

Then fling out the banner, on high let it wave
  While millions of freemen surround it ;
Our children, whenever we sink in the grave,
  Shall inherit that flag as we found it.

Neither renegade traitor, with dastardly hand,
  Nor foreign assailant shall rend it,
While an Irish-American stands on the soil
  With a heart and an arm to defend it.

Then up with the standard — up, up with the flag
  Before which proud Albion's red ensign
Trailed humbly in dust, an anath'matized rag,
  Degraded at Yorktown and Trenton.

Then up with the banner, on high let it wave,
  Hurrah ! 't is the flag of the world !
We swear before Heaven to fight and to save,
  Or to fall, while it still is unfurled.

SOUTH CAROLINA GENTLEMAN.

Air — " *The Fine Old English Gentleman.*"

DOWN in a small Palmetto State the curious
   ones may find,
A ripping, tearing gentleman, of an uncommon kind,
A staggering, swaggering sort of chap, who takes
      his whiskey straight,
And frequently condemns his eyes to that ultimate
      vengeance which a clergyman of high stand-
      ing has assured must be a sinner's fate.
This South Carolina gentleman, one of the present
      time.

You trace his genealogy, and not far back you 'll
      see,
A most undoubted octoroon, or mayhap a mustee,
And if you note the shaggy locks that cluster on
      his brow,
You 'll find that every other hair is varied with a
      kink that seldom denotes pure Caucasian
      blood, but on the contrary betrays an ad-
      mixture with a race not particularly popu-
      lar now.
This South Carolina gentleman, one of the present
      time.

He always wears a full-dress coat, pre-Adamite in
    cut,
With waistcoat of the loudest style through which
    his ruffles jut,
Six breastpins deck his horrid front, and on his fin-
    gers shine
Whole invoices of diamond rings which would
    hardly pass muster with the Original Jacobs
    in Chatham-street for jewels gen-u-ine.
This South Carolina gentleman, one of the present
    time.

He chews tobacco by the pound and spits upon the
    floor,
If there is not a box of sand behind the nearest
    door,
And when he takes his weekly spree he clears a
    mighty track,
Of everything that bears the shape of whiskey-skin,
    gin and sugar, brandy sour, peach and honey,
    irrepressible cock-tail rum, and gum, and
    luscious apple-jack.
This South Carolina gentleman, one of the present
    time.

He takes to euchre kindly, too, and plays an
    awful hand,

Especially when those he tricks his style don't
    understand,
And if he wins, why then he stoops to pocket all
    the stakes,
But if he loses, then he says to the unfortunate
    stranger who had chanced to win: "It 's
    my opinion you are a cursed abolitionist and
    if you don't leave South Carolina in one
    hour you will be hung like a dog." But no
    offer to pay his loss he makes.
This South Carolina gentleman, one of the present
    time.

Of course he 's all the time in debt to those who
    credit give,
Yet manages upon the best the market yields to live,
But if a Northern creditor asks him his bill to heed,
This honorable gentleman instantly draws two
    bowie-knives and a pistol, dons a blue
    cockade, and declares that in consequence
    of the repeated aggressions of the North,
    and its gross violations of the Constitution,
    he feels that it would utterly degrade him
    to pay any debt whatever, and that in fact
    he has at last determined to SECEDE.
This South Carolina gentleman, one of the present
    time.

SONG OF THE UNION SOLDIERS.

BY EMELINE S. SMITH.

A MIGHTY band, encamped we lie
  Upon the river's borders,
And wait, while weary weeks go by,
  Our General's marching orders,
The days are dark, the nights are drear,
  The chilling storms beat o'er us ;
And, shivering in our tents, we hear
  The winter-wind's wild chorus.

Yet though our soldier-fare is hard,
  And though our lives are dreary,
There 's not a man of all our band
  Grows discontent or weary.
We know the conquest-hour will come,
  And, strong in this assurance,
We wait, and forge in trial-fires,
  The armor of endurance.

Not lost, these seeming idle hours —
  They 're like those mystic trances
In which the winter grain awaits
  Fair Spring 's awakening glances.

The germs of valor, slumbering now,
    Will bloom on fields of glory,
And bear such fruit as long shall be
    Embalmed in song and story.

Dear are the joys we've left behind —
    Aye, dear beyond all measure,
Each sweet and sacred tie of home,
    Each holy household treasure.
But dearer far our native land —
    God's blessings rest upon her !
We proudly say we'd die to-day
    To shield her from dishonor !

Her past was bright with glorious deeds —
    Their memory still is shining
With light so clear, it warms us here,
    And hushes all repining.
In that calm " light of other days "
    Our fathers stand before us,
And tell us how to meet the ills
    That now hang darkly o'er us.

Their spirit-voices seem to float
    Above the night-wind's wailing,
And breathe, in many a thrilling note,
    Of hope and trust unfailing.

The Power that led these valiant men
   Through stormy seas of sorrow,
Can still illume our night of gloom
   With dawn of happier morrow.

Then, comrades, as we lie encamped
   Upon the river's border,
We 'll patient wait, through every fate,
   The wished-for marching-order.
We 'll keep our muskets clean and bright,
   Our pulses calm and steady,
And when the hour of action comes,
   The foe shall find us " ready."

———◆———

HYMN OF THE CONNECTICUT TWELFTH.

Tune — "*America.*"

BE Thou our country's Chief,
   In this our year of grief,
     All Father great ;
Go forth with awful tread,
Crush Treason's serpent head,
Bring back our sons misled,
     And save our State.

Uphold our Stripes and Stars
Through war's destroying jars
   With Thy right hand;
O God of battles, lead
Where our swift squadrons speed,
Where our brave brothers bleed
   For Fatherland.

Break every yoke and chain,
Let truth and justice reign
   From deep to deep;
Make all our statutes right
In Thy most holy sight;
Light us, O Lord of Light,
   Thy ways to keep.

God bless our Fatherland,
God make it strong and grand
   On sea and shore;
Ages its glory swell,
Peace in its borders dwell,
God stand its sentinel
   Forevermore.

ON ! BROTHERS, ON !

BY SARAH WARNER BROOKS.

AIR — *"Hail to the Chief."*

ON ! brothers, on ! for the flag that is peerless !
   Striped from the rainbow, and starred from
     the sky.
On, with a sturdy step ! dauntless and fearless !
  On, to unfurl it in triumph, or die !
     Honored in all the lands,
     Now shall unholy hands
  Trail it, defiled and despised, in the dust ?
     Down with the " traitor's rag ! "
     Up with the starry flag !
  Death for our banner ! and God for the just !

Fiercely at Sumter have thundered their cannon ;
  Bravely the guns of our hero replied ! —
On ! for the ashes that slumber at Vernon !
  On ! for the city whose name is our pride !
     Now let our country's guns
     Sweep down the bastard sons !
  Woe for her chivalry's flower in the dust !
     Down with the " traitor's rag ! "
     Up with the starry flag !
  Death for our banner ! and God for the just !

On, with a prayer ! there is peril before us !
  On, in the face of death, fearless and proud !
Life ! with the flag that our fathers waved over us !
  Death ! with its crimson-stained folds for a shroud !
      Now for our " fatherland,"
       Strike with true heart and hand !
Loyal our venture — and heavenward our trust !
      Down with the " traitor's rag !"
      Up with the starry flag !
Death for our banner ! and God for the just !

"I FIGHTS MIT SIGEL !"

BY GRANT P. ROBINSON.

I MET him again, he was trudging along,
  His knapsack with chickens was swelling ;
He 'd "Blenkered " these dainties, and thought it
    no wrong,
  From some secessionist's dwelling.
" What regiment 's yours ? and under whose flag
  Do you fight ? " said I, touching his shoulder ;
Turning slowly around, he smilingly said,
  For the thought made him stronger and bolder,
      " *I fights mit Sigel !*"

The next time I saw him his knapsack was gone,
  His cap and canteen were missing,
Shell, shrapnel, and grape, and the swift rifle-ball,
  Around him, and o'er him were hissing.
How are you, my friend, and where have you been,
  And for what, and for whom are you fighting?
He said, as a shell from the enemy's gun
  Sent his arm and his musket a " kiting : "
      •   " *I fights mit Sigel !* "

And once more I saw him and knelt by his side ;
  His life-blood was rapidly flowing ;
I whispered of home, wife, children, and friends,
  The bright land to which he was going ;
And have you no word for the dear ones at home,
  The " wee one," the father or mother ?
" Yaw ! yaw ! " said he, " tell them ! oh ! tell them
    I fights " —
  Poor fellow ! he thought of no other —
      " *I fights mit Sigel !* "

We scraped out a grave, and he dreamlessly sleeps
  On the banks of the Shenandoah River ;
His home or his kindred alike are unknown,
  His reward in the hands of the Giver.
We placed a rough board at the head of his grave,
  " And we left him alone in his glory,"

But on it we marked, ere we turned from the spot,
The little we knew of his story —
      " *I fights mit Sigel !* "

———◆———

SONG.

DEDICATED TO THE FIRST REGIMENT OF VERMONT.

BY ROBERT BLANC.

AIR — " *Hurrah for New England.*"

FROM woody hills and mountains bold,
  Which nought but freemen know,
Beneath their starry flag enrolled,
  They march to meet the foe.
Where giant pines and bemlocks wave
  By rock and mountain-rill,
They rise, their native land to save,
  With patriotic will.

Chorus :

Hurrah ! for you, Green-Mountain Boys,
  Ye bold, free mountaineers !
No drop of coward blood alloys,
  The heart devoid of fears.

From valley-homes, by rivers fair
  That wind among the hills,
Stern rings their tramp upon the air,
  . While ev'ry traitor thrills.
Come on, Green-Mountain Boys, come on !
  Brave sons of gallant sires !
And strike for Freedom's flag and home
  Till ev'ry foe expires.

Your mountain-air breeds stalwart frames,
  And hearts to terror sealed,
To win from fight a deathless fame,
  Or die upon the field.
Remember well the days of old !
  Remember Allen's name !
Fight ye as did your fathers bold —
  Strike for your ancient fame !

BONNIE BLUE FLAG.

BY ISAAC M. BALL.

WE 'RE fighting for our Union,
  We 're fighting for our trust ;
We 're fighting for that happy land,
  Where sleeps our father's dust.

It cannot be dissevered,
  Though it cost us bloody wars,
We ne'er can give up the land
  Where float the Stripes and Stars.
Chorus — Hurrah! hurrah!
        For equal rights, hurrah!
        Hurrah for the good old flag
        That bears the Stripes and Stars.

We treated you as brothers,
  Until you drew the sword,
With wrong impious hand at Sumter
  You cut the silver cord,
So now you hear our bugles, —
  We come, the sons of Mars;
We'll rally round that brave old flag,
  Which bears the Stripes and Stars.

We do not want your cotton,
  We care not for your slaves,
But rather than divide this land,
  We'll fill your Southern graves.
With Lincoln for our Chieftain,
  We'll wear our country's scars;
We'll rally round that brave old flag,
  Which bears the Stripes and Stars.

We deem our cause most holy,
　　We know we 're in the right;
And twenty millions of free men
　　Stand ready for the fight.
Our bride is fair Columbia,
　　No stain her beauty mars;
O'er her we 'll raise that brave old flag,
　　Which bears the Stripes and Stars.

And when this war is over,
　　We 'll each resume our homes,
And treat you still as brothers,
　　Wherever you may roam.
We 'll pledge the hand of friendship
　　And think no more of wars;
But dwell in peace beneath that flag
　　Which bears the Stripes and Stars.
　　　　Hurrah! hurrah!
　　　　For equal rights, hurrah!
　　　　Hurrah for that brave old flag
　　　　Which bears the Stripes and Stars.

11

THE LAST MAN OF BEAUFORT.*

Air — *"The Last Rose of Summer."*

'TIS the last man at Beaufort,
   Left sitting alone;
All his valiant companions
   Had " vamosed " and gone;

No secesh of his kindred
   To comfort is nigh,
And his liquor 's expended,
   The bottle is dry !

" We 'll not leave thee, thou lone one,
   Or harshly condemn —
Since your friends have all ' mizzled,'
   You can't sleep with them ;

" And it 's no joking matter
   To sleep with the dead ;
So we 'll take you back with us —
   Jim, lift up his head ! "

* On the day the town of Beaufort, S. C., was entered
by the National troops, all the inhabitants were found to
have fled, except one white man, who, being too much
intoxicated to join his compatriots in flight, had been
forced to remain behind.

He muttered some words
  As they bore him away,
And the breeze thus repeated
  The words he did say:

" When the liquor 's all out,
  And your friends they have flown,
Oh I who would inhabit
  This Beaufort alone ? "

———◆———

RALLYING SONG OF THE TENTH LEGION.*

BY A. D. DUBOIS.

WE have come from the mountains —
  We have come from the mountains —
We have come from the mountains
  Of the old Empire State,
With the Stars and Stripes above us,
And the prayers of those that love us,
Every single soldier of us
  Is prepared for any fate.

We have left our cheerful quarters
By the Hudson's smiling waters,

* New York State Volunteers.

And our wives and sons and daughters,
  For the fierce and bloody fight.
But they need not deplore us,
With the foe encamped before us,
For the God who watches o'er us,
  Will himself protect the Right.

From the Delaware we rally,
From the Mamakating Valley,
And to combat forth we sally
  When our bleeding country calls —
From the Shawangunk Mountains hoary,
And the Minisink, whose story
Tells what recompense of glory
  Waits the soldier when he falls.

From old Sullivan we muster —
She is loyal, we can trust her —
And from Orange and from Ulster,
  And from bright Cochecton's banks,
And there's plenty in those regions
For a dozen more such Legions,
All as sturdy as Norwegians,
  And prepared to fill the ranks.

Then whene'er our country needs us,
And where'er our banner leads us,

Never heeding what impedes us,
   We will follow to the death;
For the patriot must not falter,
When his country's foes assault her,
And profane her sacred altar
   With their pestilential breath.

May our flag float on forever
O'er a Union none can sever,
And may vile Secession never
   Spread its ruin through our land;
May our country's wrongs be righted,
And her children reunited,
And her flag no more be blighted
   By the touch of Treason's hand.

———✦———

OHIO, FAIR AND FREE.

BY G. W. Y.

OHIO fair, thou art to me
   More dear than all the world besides;
I love thee well from Erie's sea,
   To where thy peaceful river glides;
Ohio fair, for thee I fight,
And those in peace with thee to-night.

Though lovely skies are o'er my head,
  And charming vales beneath my feet,
Wild Southern scenes around me spread,
  With music low, enchanting, sweet—
I backward gaze, with sad regret,
To thee, my home, I can't forget.

Thy rounded hills, though often white
  With snow, or bleak mid winter's rain,
Look dear to me, thrice dear to-night,
  As I, in dreams, return again;
And loved Ohio, fair old home,
O'er boyhood's haunts in pleasure roam.

Thy valleys, rent by babbling brooks,
  Which music make the whole day long;
Thy cots, reared up in sheltered nooks,
  Where sweetly rings gay childhood's song;
These all are mine, Ohio free, ·
As mem'ry brings them back to me.

The old brown house I wept to leave,
  Beside the hills so grand and stern,
Where mother, sisters, morn and eve,
  Ask God for me a safe return,
Again is seen, as last beheld,
When sad farewells my bosom swelled.

The winding path, I know it well,
  Across the fields, along the streams,
Is trod again as heart-throbs swell,
  To meet the fond one of my dreams, —
The one, Ohio, loved by me,
As only I love her and thee.

Thus, thus, a soldier prone to dream,
  I think of scenes once loved and known,
Though miles uncounted intervene
  Between me and my dear old home.
Thus, thus, Ohio, fair and free,
A son of thine remembers thee.

Ohio, fair, thou art to me
  More dear than all the world besides,
I love thee well from Erie's sea,
  To where thy peaceful river glides;
Ohio, fair, for thee I fight,
And those in peace with thee to-night.

    HOLLY-SPRINGS, Miss.

WORDS THAT CAN BE SUNG TO THE "HALLELUJAH CHORUS."

BY HENRY H. BROWNELL.

If people *will* sing about Old John Brown, there is no reason why they should n't have words with a little meaning and rhythm in them.

OLD John Brown lies a-mouldering in the grave,
   Old John Brown lies slumbering in his
     grave —
But John Brown's soul is marching with the brave,
        His soul is marching on.
       Glory, glory, hallelujah!
       Glory, glory, hallelujah!
       Glory, glory, hallelujah!
        His soul is marching on.

He has gone to be a soldier in the army of the
   Lord,
He is sworn as a private in the ranks of the
   Lord —
He shall stand at Armageddon with his brave old
   sword —
       When Heaven is marching on
      Glory, glory, hallelujah, &c.
       For heaven is marching on.

He shall file in front where the lines of battle form,
He shall face to front when the squares of battle
    form —
Time with the column, and charge in the storm,
        Where men are marching on.
     Glory, glory, hallelujah, &c.
        True men are marching on.

Ah! foul tyrants! do ye hear him where he comes?
Ah! black traitors! do ye know him as he comes?
In thunder of the cannon and roll of the drums,
        As we go marching on.
     Glory, glory, hallelujah, &c.
        We all are marching on.

Men may die, and moulder in the dust,
Men may die, and arise again from dust,
Shoulder to shoulder, in the ranks of the just,
        When Heaven is marching on.
     Glory, glory, hallelujah, &c.
        The Lord is marching on.

April 17, 1862.

SAYS PRIVATE MAGUIRE.

BY T. B. ALDRICH.

[I must beg the pardon of Private Maguire, of the ——
New York Regiment, for thus publicly putting his senti-
ments into verse. The following lyric will assure him
that I have not forgotten how generously he shared his
scanty blanket with me, one terrible night in the Virginia
woods, when a blanket was worth fifty dollars an inch.]

I.

OCH! 'tis nate to be captain or colonel,
    Divil a bit would I want to be higher;
But to rust as a private, I think 's an infernal
    Predicament surely," says Private MAGUIRE.

II.

" *They* can go sparkin' and playin' at billiards,
    With greenbacks to spend for their slightest
        desire,
Loafin' and atin', and dbrinkin' at WILLARD'S,
    While *we're* on the pickets," says Private
        MAGUIRE.

III.

" Livin' in clover, they think it 's a thrifle
    To stand out all night in the rain and the mire,

And a Rebel hard by with a villainous rifle
   Jist ready to pop ye," says Private MAGUIRE.

IV.

" Faith, now, it 's not that I 'm afther complainin';
   I 'm spilin' to meet ye, JEFF. DAVIS, Esquire !
Ye blag-gard ! — it 's only I 'm weary of thrainin',
   And thrainin', and thrainin'," says Private
   MAGUIRE.

V.

" O Lord, for a row ! but, MAGUIRE, be aisy,
   Keep yourself sweet for the inemy's fire,
MCCLELLAN 's the saplin' that shortly will plaze ye,
   Be the holy ST. PATHRICK ! " says Private
   MAGUIRE.

VI.

" And, lad, if ye 're hit, (O, bedad, that eternal
   JIMMY O'DOWD would make up to MARIA !)
Whether ye 're sargeant, or captain, or colonel,
   Ye 'll die with the best, then ! " says Private
   MAGUIRE.

AMERICA, AMERICA!

A SONG FOR THE TIMES.

BY S. G. BULFINCH.

AMERICA, America !
   Time's youngest, brightest birth,
The hope of suffering nations,
The glory of the earth !
   For thee we raise
   To God our praise,
Whose goodness faileth never ;
   His grace divine
   Above thee shine,
And keep thee *great* forever !

America, America !
Thy cause is Freedom's own,
   Thy foe is each oppressor,
Thy king is God alone.
   For this we raise
   To him our praise,
Whose goodness faileth never ;
   His grace divine
   Upon thee shine,
And keep thee *free* forever !

America, America !
'T was justice nerved our sires,
And noble patriot feeling,
And pure devotion's fires ;
For this we raise
To God our praise,
Whose goodness faileth never ,
His grace divine
Upon thee shine,
And keep thee *true* forever.

America, America !
Our fathers left thee ONE ;
The holy tie that binds us
Was knit by Washington.
For this we raíse
To God our praise,
Whose goodness faileth never ;
His grace divine
Upon thee shine,
And keep thee ONE forever.

America, America !
No traitor's hand shall mar
The glory of thy standard,
Or blot a single star ;
And we who raise

To God our praise,
Whose goodness faileth never,
Pledge heart and hand
To keep our land
Great, free, true, one forever!
DORCHESTER, Mass., *July,* 1862.

——◆——

THE NEW BALLAD OF LORD LOVELL.*

LORD LOVELL he sat in St. Charles's Hotel,
In St. Charles's Hotel sat he,
As fine a case of a Southern swell
As ever you 'd wish to see — see — see,
As ever you 'd wish to see.

Lord Lovell the town had vowed to defend;
A-waving his sword on high,
He swore that his last ounce of powder he 'd spend,
And in the last ditch he 'd die.

He swore by black and he swore by blue,
He swore by the stars and bars,

* Mansfield Lovell, who commanded the Rebel troops
at New Orleans, and who, on the approach of the national
fleet and army to that place, "led his forces out of the
town."

That never he 'd fly from a Yankee crew
   While he was a son of Mars.

He had fifty thousand gallant men,
   Fifty thousand men had he,
Who had all sworn with him that they 'd never
   Surrender to any tarnation Yankee.

He had forts that no Yankee alive could take ;
   He had iron-clad boats a score,
And batteries all around the Lake,
   And along the river-shore.

Sir Farragut came with a mighty fleet,
   With a mighty fleet came he,
And Lord Lovell instanter began to retreat,
   Before the first boat he could see.

His fifty thousand gallant men
   Dwindled down to thousands six :
They heard a distant cannon and then
   Commenced a-cutting their sticks.

" Oh ! tarry, Lord Lovell ! " Sir Farragut cried,
   " Oh ! tarry Lord Lovell ! " said he ;
" I rather think not," Lord Lovell replied,
   " For I 'm in a great hurry."

" I like the drinks at St. Charles's Hotel,
  But I never could bear strong Porter,
Especially when it 's served on the shell,
  Or mixed in an iron mortar."

" I reckon you 're right," Sir Farragut said,
  " I reckon you 're right," said he,
" For if my Porter should fly to your head,
  A terrible smash there 'd be."

Oh ! a wonder it was to see them run,
  A wonderful thing to see,
And the Yankees sailed up without shooting a gun,
  And captured their great citie.

Lord Lovell kept running all day and night,
  Lord Lovell a-running kept he,
For he swore he could n't abide the sight
  Of the gun of a live Yankee.

When Lord Lovell's life was brought to a close
  By a sharp-shooting Yankee gunner,
From his head there sprouted a red, red nose,
  From his feet — a Scarlet Runner.

UP, BRAVE BOYS, TO "DOUBLE-QUICK TIME."

BY ELIZABETH T. PORTER BEACH.

TUNE — "*Pop goes the Weasel.*"

UP!" brave boys! to " double-quick time!"
  Foes invade our border!
Up! to music's "double-quick time!"
  To arms! to arms! in order!
Ready! boys, in double-quick time!
  Each man in his station; —
On! to save your cherished clime!
  Viva our nation!

Forward! march! to "double-quick time!"
  Forward, all, in order!
Let our "cry" in musical rhyme,
  Ring o'er the border!
Quickly it rang throughout our land,
  Echoes loud resounding;
Quickly raised a mighty band!
  Valor abounding!

Echo our war-cry, each true son,
  "Freedom, and our Nation!
12

God! our Union! Washington!
  Columbia's salvation!"
Double-quick strike! let each blow tell,
  For our preservation —
Do your duty, Northmen, well! —
  Loyal to your nation!

Let our banner triumphantly wave!
  Stars and Stripes high gleaming!
Guard it well, ye faithful brave!
  Gloriously streaming!
Double-quick strike then, for the Right!
  God! and our great nation!
He will be with the Just in fight!
  Grant them salvation!

———◆———

NEW JERSEY WAR-SONG.

BY JUDGE WHITLEY.

I'M a gallant Jersey soldier,
  Fearing neither wounds nor scar;
When in battle, none is bolder,
  Valor is my leading star.

To arms ! to arms, we cry ;
When duty calls no fear appalls ;
We 'll conquer, we 'll conquer, or we 'll nobly
    die.
Then march away, march away !
Trumpet sounds, and bugles play ;
March away, march away !
  To the martial fife and drum.

Should the Rebel hosts advancing,
  Measure swords with Jersey Blues,
Southern horsemen, gayly prancing,
  Bear ye back the dismal news :
    " Our State 's in arms " ; to arms, we cry,
    When duty calls, no fear appalls,
    We 'll conquer, we 'll conquer, or we 'll nobly
        die.
    Then march away, march away,
    Trumpet sounds and bugles play ;
    March away, march away !
      To the martial fife and drum.

ALL FORWARD !

WRITTEN FOR THE SECOND REGIMENT, CONNECTICUT VOLUNTEERS.

BY ROSE TERRY.

AIR — "*Garibaldi's Hymn.*"

ALL forward!   All forward!
All forward to battle! the trumpets are crying ;
Forward! All forward! our old flag is flying.
When Liberty calls us we linger no longer,
Rebels, come on! though a thousand to one !
Liberty! Liberty! deathless and glorious,
Under thy banner thy sons are victorious,
Free souls are valiant, and strong arms are
       stronger —
God shall go with us and battle be won.
              Hurrah for the banner!
              Hurrah for the banner!
Hurrah for our banner, the flag of the free !

       All forward!   All forward !
All forward for Freedom!   In terrible splendor
She comes to the loyal who die to defend her:
Her Stars and her Stripes o'er the wild wave of
       battle
Shall float in the heavens to welcome us on.

All forward ! to glory, though life-blood is pouring,
Where bright swords are flashing, and cannon are
     roaring ;
Welcome to death in the bullet's quick rattle —
Fighting or falling shall Freedom be won.
     Hurrah for the banner, &c.

    All forward !   All forward !
All forward to conquer ! Where free hearts are
     beating
Death to the coward who dreams of retreating !
Liberty calls us from mountain and valley ;
Waving her banner she leads to the fight.
Forward ! all forward ! the trumpets are crying,
The drum beats to arms, and our old flag is flying ;
Stout hearts and strong hands around it shall
     rally —
Forward to battle for God and the Right !
     Hurrah for the banner !
     Hurrah for the banner !
Hurrah for our banner, the flag of the free !

ARKANSIAN BATTLE-HYMN.

BY LIEUT.-COL. A. W. BISHOP.

Air — " *Marching Along.*"

ARKANSIANS are rallying round the glorious
    Stripes and Stars —
We have sworn unceasing vengeance 'gainst the
    hated stars and bars;
We know no law but justice, though covered o'er
    with scars,
        As we go marching on.
Chorus — Glory ! glory ! hallelujah,
        Glory ! glory ! hallelujah,
        Glory ! glory ! hallelujah,
           As we go marching on.

We were driven from our homes, our wives, and
    children dear ;
Our native hills and valleys no longer gave us
    cheer —
But now, thank God ! forever, we once again are
    here,
        Where the war goes bravely on.
      Glory, glory, hallelujah, &c.

We remember David Walker, who sought our votes
 of old,
And linked to ours his " destiny," in voice of
 utt'rance bold,
But southward drove his " contrabands," a bid for
 Rebel gold,
> As we came marching on.
> Glory, glory, hallelujah, &c.

We scorn deception ever, we scorn it most of
 all
In the proud and haughty Rebels, who are seeking still our fall —
But soon they 'll hear the shouting, and the trumpet's gath'ring call,
> As we go marching on.
> Glory, glory, hallelujah, &c.

We 've fought, bled, and suffered, but gladly sprung
 to arms,
 To trample out the treason that desolates our
 farms ;
We 'll bear aloft our banner, and to peace restore
 her charms,
> As we go marching on.
> Glory, glory, hallelujah, &c.

Let the Union of the fathers be the Union ever-
    more,
Of the sons and the daughters of those who fought
    of yore ;
And moving on the Arkansas, we 'll strike the far-
    ther shore,
        As we go marching on.
        Glory, glory, hallelujah, &c.

Then JUBILATE DEO ! let the welkin ever ring
With the joyous shouts of freemen, attendant now
    on spring,
And hosannahs loudly shout to God alone, our
    King,
        As we go marching on.
        Glory, glory, hallelujah, &c.

ARMY-HYMN.

BY OLIVER WENDELL HOLMES.

" Old Hundred."

O LORD of Hosts ! Almighty King !
    Behold the sacrifice we bring !
To every arm Thy strength impart,
Thy spirit shed through every heart !

Wake in our breasts the living fires,
The holy faith that warmed our sires;
Thy hand hath made our Nation free:
To die for her is serving Thee.

Be Thou a pillared flame to show
The midnight snare, the silent foe;
And when the battle thunders loud,
Still guide us in its moving cloud.

God of all nations! Sovereign Lord!
In thy dread name we draw the sword,
We lift the starry flag on high
That fills with light our stormy sky.

From Treason's rent, from Murder's stain
Guard Thou its folds till Peace shall reign, —
Till fort and field, till shore and sea
Join our loud anthem, PRAISE TO THEE!

THE FALL OF VICKSBURG.

BY WILLIAM ROSS WALLACE.

I.

"POWER, Power, Power!" sing;
  Mighty Cotton is the King:
Armed with dungeon, lash, and rack,
Bleeding subjects at his back,
How he laughs their groans to scorn;
They for him alone were born —
          " *Cotton's King!*"

II.

So the brutal despots cried,
Storming in their Godless pride;
Honor, mercy, never known,
Justice on a shattered throne,
And the only chorus — "Might,
With his red arm gives the Right —
          " *Cotton's King!*"

III.

Hark! there is another cry:
How it sweeps a tempest by!
See, a Nation fire-eyed stands,
Freedom's Charter in her hands!

See, the despots storm no more,
While the guns on VICKSBURG roar,
    " GOD *is King !* "

IV.

" Wreaths for GRANT and PORTER !" shout ;
Fling our flag, a star-storm, out :
Honor has *not* left the clime ;
Justice sweeps the harp of Time,
Shaking all the ransomed shore,
While the guns on VICKSBURG roar,
    " GOD *is King!* "

V.

Nations, join the joyous cry !
Worlds, that shuddered in the sky
As ye looked down on the chain
Clanking over Earth and Main,
Shout " The reign of Hell is o'er !"
While the guns on VICKSBURG roar,
Over ruthless VICKSBURG roar,
Over *fallen* VICKSBURG roar,
    " GOD IS KING !"

LITTLE RHODY.

O F all the true host that New England can boast,
    From down by the sea unto highland,
. No State is more true, or more willing to do,
    Then dear little Yankee Rhode Island.
          Loyal and true little Rhody !
          Bully for you ! little Rhody ;
Governor Sprague was not very vague,
When he said, " Shoulder Arms ! Little Rhody ! "

Not backward at all at the President's call,
    Nor yet with the air of a toady ;
The gay little State, not a moment too late,
    Sent soldiers to answer for Rhody.
          Loyal and true little Rhody !
          Bully for you ! little Rhody ;
Governor Sprague was not very vague,
When he said, " Shoulder Arms ! Little Rhody."

Two regiments raised, and by ev'ry one praised,
    Were soon on the march for head-quarters ;
All furnished first-rate at the cost of their State,
    And regular fighting dread-naughters !
          Loyal and true little Rhody,
          Bully for you ! little Rhody ;

Governor Sprague was not very vague,
When he said, " Shoulder Arms ! Little Rhody."

Let traitors look out, for there 's never a doubt
　That Uncle Abe's army will trip 'em ;
And as for the loud Carolinian crowd,
　Rhode Island, alone, sir, can whip 'em !
　　　　　Loyal and true little Rhody !
　　　　　Bully for you ! little Rhody ;
Governor Sprague is a very good egg,
And worthy to lead little Rhody !

———◆———

THE YEAR OF JUBILEE.

SAY, darkies, hab you seen de massa,
　Wid de muffstash on his face,
Go 'long de road some time dis mornin,'
　Like he 's going to leave de place ?
He seen de smoke way up de ribber
　Where de Lincum gunboats lay ;
He took his hat and left berry sudden,
　And I 'spose he 's runned away.
　　　　De massa run, ha! ha !
　　　　De darkey stay, ho ! ho !
　　　　It mus' be now de kingdum comin,'
　　　　An' de yar ob Jubilo.

He 's six foot one way and two foot todder,
  An' he weighs six hundred poun',
His coat 's so big he could n't pay de tailor,
  An' it won't reach half way roun',
He drills so much dey calls him cap'n,
  An' he gits so mighty tan'd,
I spec he 'll try to fool dem Yankees
  For to tink he 's contraband.
        De massa run, ha! ha!
          De darkey stay, ho! ho!
        It mus' be now de kingdum comin,
          An' the yar of Jubilo.

De darkies got so lonesome libb'n
  In de log hut on de lawn,
Dey move dere tings into massa's parlor
  For to keep it while he 's gone.
Dar 's wine and cider in de kichin,
  And de darkies dey hab some,
I spec it will all be 'fiscated,
  When de Lincum sojers come.
        De massa run, ha! ha!
          De darkey stay, ho! ho!
        It mus' be now de kingdum comin,'
          An' de yar ob Jubilo.

De oberseer, he makes us trubble,
  An' he dribes us roun' a spell,

We lock him up in de smoke-house cellar,
  Wid de key flung in de well.
De whip is lost, de han'-cuff broke,
  But de massa hab his pay,
He 's big and ole enough for to know better
  Dan to went an' run away.
      De massa run, ha! ha!
       De darkey stay, ho! ho!
      It mus' be now de kingdum comin,'
      An' de yar ob Jubilo.

———◆———

"O! STONEMAN 'S UP AND AWAY, BOYS."

Air — "*O, Kenmure's on and awa.*"

OH! Stoneman 's up and away, boys,
  Oh! Stoneman 's up and away!
And side by side, behind him ride,
  Three thousand gallants gay.
Success to Stoneman's raid, boys,
  Success to horse and man;
From Rapidan to furthest James,
  And back to Rapidan!

Here 's Stoneman's health in wine, boys;
   Here 's all their healths in wine;
For fear and woe shall strike the foe,
   Where'er their sabres shine.
For all his men are picked, boys,
   And all his lads are men;
Their hearts and swords are metal true,
   And each is good for ten!

They 'll live or die with fame, boys,
   They 'll live or die with fame;
In after years, with pride and tears,
   Shall mothers tell their name.
But they 'll come safely back, boys,
   But they 'll come safely back;
Oh! they 'll come back, though fire and blood
   Shall surge around their track!

FREEDOM'S LAND.

DEDICATED TO THE HEROES OF ANTIETAM.

BY W. W. ELY, M. D.

TUNE — "*Dixie.*"

LET others praise the land of cotton,
  Nigger-slaves and treason rotten;
Cheer away, cheer away, cheer away, Freedom's
  land:
We'll sing the land where we were born,
Where honest toil no man dares scorn:
Cheer away, cheer away, cheer away, Freedom's
  land.
Chorus — Although from home we sever, away,
    away,
      We'll never sigh, but live and die,
    True to our cause forever, Hooray!
  •   Hooray!
      True to our cause forever.

In the good old times, our fathers fought
To leave us treasures dearly bought;
      Cheer away, &c.
    13

At duty's call our armies come,
To strike confederate Rebels dumb;
        Cheer away! &c.
        Although from home we sever, &c.

The haughty South, to her own undoing,
Our country seeks to rule or ruin;
        Cheer away! &c.
Maddened alike with pride and whiskey,
They 'll find their foolish war too risky;
        Cheer away! &c.
        Although from home we sever, &c.

Our noble boys are bravely battling,
Where the deadly balls are rattling;
        Cheer away! &c.
Though they may fall, they 'll never fail,
Their iron hearts shall never quail;
        Cheer away! &c.
        Although from home we sever, &c.

While Uncle SAM needs a defender,   •
The loyal North will ne'er surrender;
        Cheer away! &c.
With charging steel and dashing saddle,
We 've learned to make the Rebs skedaddle;
        Cheer away! &c.
        Although from home we sever, &c.

Then let us ever, living, dying,
Be where the Stars and Stripes are flying;
   Cheer away! &c.
The good old flag we 'll never alter,
And he who would, deserves a halter;
   Cheer away! &c.
   Although from home we sever, &c.

" GREENBACKS."

GREEN be thy back upon thee!
 Thou pledge of happier days,
When bloody-handed Treason
 No more its hand shall raise;
But still, from Maine to Texas,
 The Stars and Stripes shall wave,
O'er the hearts and homes of freemen,
 Nor mock one fettered slave.

Pledge — of the people's credit,
 To carry on the war,
By furnishing the sinews
 In a currency at par —
With cash enough left over,
 When they 've cancelled every note,

To buy half the thrones of Europe,
  With the crowns tossed in to boot.

Pledge — to our buried fathers,
  That sons of patriot-sires,
On Freedom's sacred altars,
  Relight their glorious fires —
That fortune, life, and honor
  To our country's cause we give —
Fortune and life may perish,
  Yet the Government shall live.

Pledge — to our unborn children,
  That, free from blot or stain,
The flag hauled down at Sumter,
  Shall yet float free again —
And, cleansed from foul dishonor,
  And rebaptized in blood,
Wave o'er the land forever,
  To Freedom and to God!

A YANKEE SOLDIER'S SONG.

I HARKENED to the thund'ring noise,
  And wondered what 't was for, sir !
But when I heard 'em tell our boys,
  I started up and swore, sir.
      Yankee boys will fight it out !
        Yankees brave and handy !
      Freedom be our battle-shout !
        Yankee doodle dandy !

They said that traitors tore our flag,
  Down there in Dixie's land, sir,
I always loved the striped rag,
  And swore by it to stand, sir.
      Yankee boys will fight it out ! &c.

I knew them Southern chaps, high-bred,
  Had called us " mud-sills " here, sir :
If on these sills they try to tread,
  I guess 't will cost them dear, sir.
      Yankee boys will fight it out ! &c.

Down South I marched, rat-tat-a-plan,
  With heart brimful of pluck, sir ;

I held my head up like a man ;
   A righteous cause brings luck, sir.
      Yankee boys will fight it out ! &c.

So proud was I of fatherland,
   Where humans all are free, sir,
I found it hard to understand
   Some things I lived to see, sir.
      Yankee boys will fight it out ! &c.

To us one day a brown man came,
   In Dixie's land a slave, sir,
And pleaded hard, in Freedom's name,
   That him we 'd try to save, sir.
      Yankee boys will fight it out ! &c.

Of course we will, our men cried out ;
   All free beneath this flag, sir !
Then he began, with hearty shout,
   To cheer the starry rag, sir.
      Yankee boys will fight it out ! &c.

But, whip in hand, a master came,
   And drove that man away, sir ;
We felt it was a burning shame,
   But could not have our say, sir.
      Yankee boys will fight it out ! &c.

To us it seems a coward's shirk —
  It makes us feel less brave, sir —
We call it mean and " mud-sill " work,
  This sending back a slave, sir !
        Yankee boys will fight it out ! &c.

We did not leave our homes to do
  Such dirty jobs as these, sir —
Our hearts within us, warm and true,
  It chills and makes 'em freeze, sir.
        Yankee boys will fight it out ! &c.

The man who works with heart is strong —
  And right keeps up the pluck, sir —
We cannot feel so bold for wrong —
  We cannot hope for luck, sir.
        Yankee boys will fight it out ! &c.

We long to have our flag unfurled
  To make the *whole* land free, sir —
For we can proudly face the world,
  When we that day shall see, sir.
        Yankee boys will fight it out ! &c.

O, how we 'll hail our banner then !
  Its fame all clear and bright, sir ;
When all can feel that they are men,
  And all have equal right, sir.

Yankee boys will fight it out !
Yankees brave and handy !
Freedom be our battle-shout !
Yankee doodle dandy !

———◆———

THE IRISH PICKET.

BY " BARNEY."

Aᴵʀ — " *I'm sitting on the stile, Mary.*"

I 'M shtanding in the mud, Biddy,
  With not a spalpeen near,
And silence, spaichless as the grave,
  Is all the sound I hear.
Me goon is at a showlder-arms,
  I 'm wetted to the bone,
And whin I 'm afther sphakin' out,
  I find meself alone.

This Southern climate 's quare, Biddy,
  A quare and bastely thing,
Wid winter absint all the year,
  And summer in the spring.
Ye mind the hot place down below ?
  And may ye never fear
I 'd dthraw comparisons — but then
  It 's awful warrum here.

The only moon I see, Biddy,
  Is one shmall star, asthore,
And that 's fornint the very cloud
  It was behind before;
The watch-fires glame along the hill
  That's swellin' to the south,
And whin the sintry passes them,
  I see his ougly mouth.

It 's dead for shlape I am, Biddy,
  And dramein' shwate I 'd be,
If them ould Rebels over there
  Would only lave me free;
But when I lane against a shtump
  And shtrive to get repose,
A musket ball be 's comin' shtraight
  To hit me spacious nose.

It 's ye I 'd like to see, Biddy,
  A shparkin here wid me,
And then, avourneen, hear ye say,
  " Acushla — Pat — machree ! "
" Och, Biddy, darlint," then says I,
  Says you, " get out of that,"
Says I, " me arrum mates your waist,"
  Says you, " Be daycent, Pat."

And how 's the pigs and ducks, Biddy ?
　　It 's them I think of shure,
That looked so innocent and shwate
　　Upon the parlor-flure ;
I 'm shure ye 're aisy with the pig,
　　That 's fat as he can be,
And fade him wid the best, because
　　I 'm towld he looks like me.

Whin I come home again, Biddy,
　　A sargent tried and thrue,
It 's joost a daycent house I 'll build,
　　And rint it chape to you.
We 'll have a parlor, bedroom, hall,
　　A duck-pond nately done,
With kitchen, pig-pen, praty-patch,
　　And garret — all in one.

But, murther ! there 's a baste, Biddy,
　　That 's crapin' round a tree,
And well I know the cratur 's there
　　To have a shot at me.
Now, Misther Rebel, say yere pray'rs,
　　And howld yer dirty paw,
Here goes ! — be jabers, Biddy, dear,
　　I 've broke his oogly jaw !

NEW ENGLAND.

BY J. O. BLYTHE, M. D.

I LOVE thee well, New England,
  Thy breath is sweet to me,
As perfume off the vineyards,
  Or spices from the sea;
As sunlight to the vision,
  Or music in the ear,
As health to all the living,
  Or joy's enraptured tear.
Chorus — Then up! and still, New England,
    Be Liberty! thy cry,
    And while a *heart* still beateth,
    Freedom shall never die.

I love thee well, New England,
  My heart is on thy hills,
Among thy rugged mountains,
  Beside the rippling rills;
Along thy rushing rivers,
  Beneath the silver pines,
Upon thy liquid lakelets,
  Margined by purple vines.
    Then up! and still, New England,
    Be Liberty! thy cry,

And while a *mountain* standeth,
Freedom shall never die.

I love thee well, New England,
  Thy craggy peaks are free!
And there the soaring eagle
  Enjoys his liberty;
There thy brave sons and daughters,
  Unshackled by a chain,
Worship at Freedom's altars,
  And sanctify their slain.
     Then up! and still, New England,
      Be Liberty! thy cry,
    And while *an eagle* soareth,
     Freedom shall never die.

Thy heroes wide lie scattered
  O'er all the hallowed soil,
Genius, and birth, and learning,
  With honest sons of toil;
Then up! and still, New England,
  Be Liberty! thy cry,
And while a *hero* breatheth,
  Freedom shall never die.

THE BANNER OF THE SKY.

BY E. P. WORTH.

OUR flag from heaven still waves,
  Set up by Him who saves,
    Enthroned above.
Arch of those beauteous rays,
Whose light forever plays
O'er all our clouded days,
    Emblem of love.
  Chorus — The rainbow-flag afar
        Shall float from shore to shore,
          In beauty evermore,
              Forevermore.

Our banner of the sky,
Formed of the light on high,
      Celestial sign ;
Ensign of liberty
For all the God made free,
Bright pledge of unity,
      From heaven to man.

Standard of victory,
Over earth's misery,
      Triumphant sign

That the eternal word
By all shall yet be heard,
Moving to sweet accord,
    With peace divine.

MARCHING SONG OF THE FIRST ARKANSAS.*

OH! we're de bully soldiers ob de " First of
    Arkansas,"
We are fightin' for de Union, we are fightin' for de
    law,
We can hit a Rebel furder dan a white man eber
    saw,
        As we go marchin' on.
        Glory, glory, hallelujah, &c.

See dar! above de centre, where de flag is wavin
    bright;

* This song was written by Captain Lindley Miller, of
the First Arkansas Colored Regiment. Captain Miller
says the " boys " sing the song on dress-parade with an
effect which can hardly be described; and ho adds that,
" while it is not very conservative, it will do to fight
with."

We are goin' out of slavery; we are bound for
    Freedom's light,
We mean to show Jeff. Davis how de Africans can
    fight!
        As we go marchin' on.

We hab done wid hoein' cotton, we hab done wid
    hoein' corn,
We are colored Yankee soldiers now, as sure as
    you are born;
When de massas hear us yellin' dey'll tink its Ga-
    briel's horn,
        As we go marchin' on.

Dey will hab to pay us wages, de wages ob their
    sin,
Dey will hab to bow their foreheads to their col-
    ored kith and kin,
Dey will hab to gib us house-room, or de roof shall
    tumble in!
        As we go marchin' on.

We heard de proclamation, massa hush it as he will;
De bird he sing it to us, hoppin' on de cotton-hill,
And de possum up de gum-tree, he could n't keep
    it still,
        As he went climbing on.

Dey said, "Now colored bredren, you shall be for-
    ever free,
From de first ob January, eighteen hundred sixty-
    three;"
We heard it in de riber goin' rushin' to de sea,
        As it went soundin' on.

Father Abraham has spoken, and de message has
    been sent,
De prison-doors he opened, and out de pris'ners
    went,
To join de sable army ob de " African descent,"
        As we go marchin' on.

Den fall in, colored bredren, you'd better do it
    soon ;
Don't you hear de drum a beatin' de Yankee
    Doodle tune ?
We are wid you now dis mornin', we'll be far
    away at noon,
        As we go marchin' on.

A SOLDIER'S PSALM OF WOMAN.

WRITTEN BY AN ILLINOIS SOLDIER AT CHATTANOOGA.

DOWN all the shining lapse of days,
   That grow and grow forever
In truer love and broader praise
   Of the Almighty Giver;
Whatever Godlike impulses
   Have blossomed in the human,
The most divine and fair of these
   Sprung from the soul of woman.

Her heart it is preserves the flower
   Of sacrificial duty,
Which, blown across the blackest hour,
   Transfigures it to beauty.
Her hands that streak these solemn years
   With vivifying graces,
And clasp the foreheads of our fears
   With light from higher places.

O, wives and mothers, sanctified
   By holy consecrations,
Turning our weariness aside,
   With blessed ministrations!
14

O, maidens, in whose dewy eyes,
   Perennial comforts glitter,
Untangling war's dark mysteries,
   And making sweet the bitter :

In desolate paths, or dangerous posts,
   By places which, to-morrow,
Shall be unto these bannered hosts
   Aceldamas of sorrow,
We hear the sound of helping feet, —
   We feel your soft caressings ;
And all our life starts up to greet
   Your lovingness with blessings !

On cots of pain, on beds of woe,
   Where stricken heroes languish,
Wan faces smile and sick hearts grow
   Triumphant over anguish.
While souls that starve in lonely gloom,
   Flush green with odorous praises ;
And all the lowly pallets bloom
   With Gratitude's white daisies.

O, lips, that from our wounds have sucked
   The fever and the burning !
O, tender fingers, that have plucked
   The madness from our mourning !

O, hearts, that beat so loyal-true,
 For soothing and for saving —
God send our hopes back unto you,
 Crowned with immortal having!

Thank God. O, Love! whereby we know
 Beyond our little seeing,
And feel serene compassions flow
 Around the ache of being;
Lo! clear o'er all the pain and dread
 Of our most sore affliction,
The sacred wings of Peace are spread
 In brooding benediction.

———◆———

THE CHILDREN OF THE BATTLE-FIELD.

BY JAMES G. CLARKE.

UPON the field of Gettysburg
 The summer sun was high,
When Freedom met her haughty foe
 Beneath a Northern sky:
Among the heroes of the North,
 Who swelled her grand array,

And rushed, like mountain eagles forth,
   From happy homes away,
There stood a man of humble fame,
   A sire of children three,
And gazed, within a little frame,
   Their pictured forms to see ;
And blame him not if in the strife
   He breathed a soldier's prayer,
"O ! Father, shield the soldier's wife,
   And for his children care."

Upon the field of Gettysburg,
   When morning shone again,
The crimson cloud of battle burst
   In streams of fiery rain :
Our legions quelled the awful flood
   Of shot, and steel, and shell ;
While banners, marked with ball and blood,
   Around them rose and fell.
And none more nobly won the name
   Of Champion for the Free,
Than he who pressed the little frame
   That held his children three ;
And none were braver in the strife,
   Than he who breathed the prayer :
"O ! Father, shield the soldier's wife,
   And for his children care."

Upon the field of Gettysburg
  The full moon slowly rose;
She looked, and saw ten thousand brows
  All pale in death's repose.
And down beside a silver stream,
  From other forms away,
Calm as a warrior in a dream,
  Our fallen comrade lay ;
His limbs were cold, his sightless eyes
  Were fixed upon the three
Sweet stars that rose in memory's skies,
  To light him o'er death's sea.
Then honored be the soldier's life,
  And hallowed be his prayer :
" O ! Father, shield the soldier's wife,
  And for his children care."

HYMN OF THE CORPS D'AFRIQUE.

BY J. C. HAGEN.

TUNE—*"Hail to the Chief."*

GLORY to God, who our fetters has broken!
  Filled be our hearts with thanksgiving and
    praise!
Glory to God for the word He has spoken —
  The word that to freemen a people can raise;
      Giving us strength and will
      Bravely our place to fill,
Till none so blind but our manhood can see;
      Teaching the traitor throng,
      Blasting the earth so long,
All in God's image made shall be free!

Proudly the star-spangled banner waves o'er us;
  Dark though the deeds 'neath its folds to us done,
Now like an angel of promise before us,
  Cheering us onward, it gleams in the sun.
      Never again to wave
      Over the hapless slave,
Terror of tyrants for aye it shall be;
      All 'neath its folds who dwell
      Shall the glad tidings tell —
Where that blessed banner floats, man is free!

Victory awaits us, for God has decreed it,
  Countless and strong though the foes that assail;
Scoffers revile us, but little we heed it;
  Ours is the truth, and the truth must prevail.
      Firm as a rock we stand,
      Guarding some sea-girt land;
Pledged heart and hand, Freedom's champions are
      we,
      Never to cease the strife
      While we have breath of life,
Till all can proudly say, " We are free ! "

A CHEER FOR THE WEST.

BY PARK BENJAMIN.

HURRAH for the glorious West !
  She has turned out the bravest and best,
  And Victory follows her arms ;
How they poured forth their volleys of fire,
While the bright, starry banners rose higher
  In the midst of the battle's alarms.

Fort Donelson's ramparts are down,
And so are her men of renown,
  Those leaders of fury and fright —

They are carried off captives or slain,
Or, fugitives over the plain,
   Escape from the terrible fight.

Hurrah for the bold General Grant!
He knew no such phrase as " I can't,"
   But uttered in thunder, " I will " —
" Move onward," " Move onward ! " — the land
Echoed wide to that word of command,
   And, hark ! it reverberates still.

Oh, perish, ye traitors and knaves,
Ye changers of men into slaves,
   Ye Rebels, so craven and base —
Where now is your boasted reliance,
And where are your scowls of defiance,
   'Mid clouds of defeat and disgrace.

The dastards and wretches who fled,
By the thief of Virginia led,
   May tell of the capture and shame
Of their brothers-in-arms who contended
Till the hot, bloody contest was ended,
   And the West won her laurels of fame.

The West ! the victorious West !
With praises and thanks she is blest,

She has crushed with invincible might
This war of Rebellion to dust ;
And she will do more if she must
And hers is the glory by right.

———◆———

THE FIGHT ABOVE THE CLOUDS.

BY WM. ROSS WALLACE.

FOR that wondrous battle-shout,
    Where beyond the tempest's rout,
With his sword and Freedom's flags,
Flashing o'er the mountain-crags
And his grand eyes all a-glow,
On the mocking Rebel foe,
Rushed the feerless " Fighting Joe " —
        In the fight above the clouds !

Nature's thunder roared beneath,
Through the morning's misty wreath
But a grander thunder rolled
Through the traitor's mountain-hold
From the heart of " Fighting Joe " —
When, like fire from below,
Swept our host upon the foe —
        In the fight above the clouds !

And still up, still up they leap,
Over chasm, rock, and steep!
Hark! the Hero's eagle-cry,
" Such as ye insult God's sky!
To your foul nests down below,
Every perjured Rebel foe!"
Cries the awful " Fighting Joe "—
  In the fight above the clouds!

How they wavered, how they fled,
How the trumpet's triumph spread,
How the Union's flag unfurled
With its Star-Hope o'er the world,
Let the nation, all a-glow,
Shout to friend and shout to foe,
While it laurels " Fighting Joe "—
  For his fight above the clouds!

O, all ye who for us fell
Far above the common dell,
Too sublimely there ye sleep
For a single eye to weep;
While in answer to each foe,
With his grand eyes all a-glow,
Points your General, " Fighting Joe "—
  To his fight above the clouds!

For that wondrous battle-shout,
Far above the tempest's rout !
'T is the symbol of the time,
When on Freedom's mount sublime,
Our Old Union shall have place
With an everlasting base,
Proudly scorning fraud and foe,
While through every cycle's flow
Nations bless our " Fighting Joe " —
    For his fight above the clouds !

———◆———

PADDY ON SAMBO AS A SOLDIER.

BY PRIVATE MILES O'REILLY.

AIR — " *The Low-Backed Car.*"

SOME tell us 't is a burning shame
  To make the naygurs fight ;
An' that the thrade of bein' kilt
  Belongs but to the white ;
But as for me, upon my sowl !
  So liberal are we here,
I 'll let Sambo be murdered in place of myself
  On every day in the year !

On every day in the year, boys,
  And every hour in the day,
The right to be kilt I 'll divide wid him,
  An' divil a word I 'll say.

In battle's wild commotion
  I should n't all object
If Sambo's body should stop a ball
  That was comin' for me direct ;
And the prod of a Southern bagnet,
  So liberal are we here,
I 'll resign and let Sambo take it
  On every day in the year !
    On every day in the year, boys,
      And wid none of your nasty pride,
    All my right in a Southern bagnet prod
      Wid Sambo I 'll divide.

The men who object to Sambo,
  Should take his place and fight ;
And it 's better to have a naygur's hue
  Than a liver that 's wake an' white ;
Though Sambo's black as the ace of spades,
  His finger a thrigger can pull,
And his eye runs straight on the barrel-sights
  From under his thatch of wool !

So hear me all, boys, darlings,
 Don't think I 'm tippin' you chaff,
The right to be killed I 'll divide wid him,
 And give him the largest half!

———◆———

GENERAL LEE'S WOOING.

AIR—"*My Maryland! My Maryland!*"

MY Maryland! My Maryland!
 Among thy hills of blue
I wander far, I wander wide,
 A lover born and true;
I sound my horn upon the hills,
 I sound it in the vale,
But echo only answers it, —
 An echo like a wail.

My Maryland! My Maryland!
 I bring thee presents fine, —
A dazzling sword with jewelled hilt,
 A flask of Bourbon wine;
I bring thee sheets of ghostly white
 To dress thy bridal bed,
With curtains of the purple eve
 And garlands gory red.

My Maryland ! My Maryland !
  Sweet land upon the shore,
Bring out thy stalwart yeomanry !
  Make clean the threshing-floor ;
My ready wains lie stretching far
  Across the fertile plain,
And I among the reapers stand
  To gather in the grain.

My Maryland ! My Maryland !
  I fondly wait to see
Thy banner flaunting in the breeze
  Beneath the trysting tree ;
While all my gallant company
  Of gentlemen, with spurs,
Come tramping, tramping o'er the hills,
  And tramping through the furze.

My Maryland ! My Maryland !
  I feel the leaden rain !
I see the winged messenger
  Come hurling to my brain !
I feathered with thy golden hair,
  'T is feathered not in vain ;
I spurn the hand that loosed the shaft,
  And curse thee in my pain.

My Maryland ! My Maryland !
  Alas ! the ruthless day !
That sees my gallant buttonwoods
  Ride galloping away ;
And ruthless for my chivalry,
  Proud gentlemen, with spurs,
Whose bones lie stark upon the hills,
  And stark among the furze.

———◆———

THE CAMP WAR-SONG.*

R AISE the banner, raise it high, boys,
    Let it float against the sky ;
" God be with us ! " this our cry, boys —
    Under it we 'll do or die.
1st. *Chorus* — Arise to glory, glory, glory,
              Our country calls — march on ! march
              on !
2d. *Chorus* — Co-ca-che-lunk-che-lunk-che-la-ly,
              Co-ca-che-lunk-che-lunk-che-lay,
              Co-ca-che-lunk-che-lunk-che-la-ly,
              Rig-a-ge-dig, and away we go!

* The version sung in the Army of the Mississippi.

Rebel miscreants, stand from under!
  Ye who bear the traitor's name!
Every star's a bolt of thunder —
  Every stripe, a living flame!
    Arise, &c.

By our patriot sires in glory —
  By our sainted WASHINGTON —
We will fight, till every Tory
  Falls, that breathes beneath the sun!
    Arise, &c.

By our homes, our hearths, and altars —
  By our sweethearts, children, wives —
He who from our Union falters,
  Dies, hath he a thousand lives!
    Arise, &c.

Under GRANT, our valiant leader,
  We will lay the traitors low;
Crushed to earth, each vile seceder
  Soon shall to our vengeance bow.
    Arise, &c.

ABRAHAM! thy name shall cheer us
  'Mid the war-field's bloody strife;

Old Fort Sumter yet shall hear us
 Call her battlements to life !
  Arise, &c.

God of battles ! we implore thee —
 Nerve our souls — make strong our arms ;
Bless us as we bow before thee,
 In the midst of war's alarms.

 Our spangled banner waving o'er us,
  We come — avengers of the free !
 Shout, boys, shout ! the foe 's before us !
  Union — God — and Liberty !
1st. Chorus — Arise to glory, glory, glory,
   Our country calls — march on ! march
   on !
2d. Chorus — Co-ca-che-lunk-che-lunk-che-la-ly,
   Co-ca-che-lunk-che-lunk-che-lay,
   Co-ca-che-lunk-che-lunk-che-la-ly,
   Rig-a-ge-dig, and away we go !

THE LASS OF THE PAMUNKY.

YOUR "glens" and "groves" I ne'er ad-
        mired,
    And O your "broom" and "birks," they pall
        so !
Of Burn sides (all but one) I 'm tired,
    And of your "bonny lasses," also.
The man that sings the "Banks of Doon,"
    And braes — I hold him but a donkey ;
My heart beats to another tune,
    And that 's the Banks of the Pamunky.

For that famed "Lass of Pattie's Mill "
    I would n't give one nickel penny ;
Of " Nannies " we 've quite had our fill,
    Of " Peggies " and of " Jessies " many ;
Ditto the " Lass of Ballochmyle,"
    All set so tediously to one key ;
Suppose we try a different style,
    And sing the Lass of the Pamunky !

Then sing no more the " Banks of Cree,"
    Or " Afton's " green and softly rounded,
But sing the steamer on the P——,
    Where they took me when I was wounded.

And sing the maiden, kind and true,
  Trim, handy, quiet, sweet, and spunky,
That nursed me, and made no ado,
  When I lay sick on the Pamunky.

Fair hands! but not too nice or coy
  To soothe my pangs with service tender;
Soft eyes! that watched a wasted boy,
  All loving, as your land's defender!
O, I was then a wretched shade,
  But now I'm strong, and growing chunky;
So, forward! but God bless the maid
  That saved my life on the Pamunky.

F. J. O.

—◆—

THE BATTLE-CRY OF FREEDOM.

YES, we'll rally round the flag, boys,
    We'll rally once again,
Shouting the battle-cry of Freedom;
We will rally from the hill-side,
We will rally from the plain,
Shouting the battle-cry of Freedom.
            Chorus:
  The Union forever! Hurrah, boys, hurrah!
  Down with the Traitors, up with the Stars;

While we rally round the flag, boys,
Rally once again,
Shouting the battle-cry of Freedom.

We are springing to the call
Of our brothers gone before,
Shouting the battle-cry of Freedom;
And we 'll fill the vacant ranks
With a million freemen more,
Shouting the battle-cry of Freedom.
    The Union forever, &c.

We will welcome to our number
The loyal, true, and brave,
Shouting the battle-cry of Freedom;
And although he may be poor
He shall never be a slave,
Shouting the battle-cry of Freedom.
    The Union forever, &c.

We are springing to the call,
From the East and from the West,
Shouting the battle-cry of Freedom;
And we 'll hurl the Rebel crew
From the land we love the best,
Shouting the battle-cry of Freedom.
    The Union forever, &c.

We are marching to the field, boys,
Going to the fight,
Shouting the battle-cry of Freedom;
And we 'll bear the glorious Stars
Of the Union and the Right,
Shouting the battle-cry of Freedom.
　The Union forever, &c.

We 'll meet the Rebel host, boys,
With fearless hearts and true,
Shouting the battle-cry of Freedom;
And we 'll show what Uncle Sam,
Has for loyal men to do,
Shouting the battle-cry of Freedom.
　The Union forever, &c.

If we fall amid the fray, boys,
We will face them to the last,
Shouting the battle-cry of Freedom;
And our comrades brave shall hear us,
As we are rushing past,
Shouting the battle-cry of Freedom.
　The Union forever, &c.

Yes, for Liberty and Union,
We are springing to the fight,
Shouting the battle-cry of Freedom;

And the victory shall be ours,
Forever rising in our might,
Shouting the battle-cry of Freedom.
The Union forever, &c.

———◆———

CAVALRY-SONG.

BY CHARLES GODFREY LELAND.

WEAPONED well, to war we ride,
    With sabres ringing by our side —
The warning-knell of death to all,
Who hold the holiest cause in thrall;
    The sacred Right
    Which grows to Might,
The day which dawns in blood-red light.

Weaponed well, to war we ride,
To conquer, tide what may betide,
For never yet, beneath the sun,
Was battle by the devil won;
    For what to thee
    Defeat may be,
Time makes a glorious victory.

Weaponed well, to war we ride —
Who braves the battle wins the bride ;
Who dies the death for Truth, shall be
Alive in love eternally :
    Though dead he lies,
    Soft, starry eyes
Smile hope to him from purple skies.

Weaponed well, to war we ride —
Hurrah ! for the surging thunder-tide,
When the cannon's roar makes all seem large,
And the war-horse screams in the crashing charge,
    And the rider strong,
    Whom he bears along,
Is a death-dart shot at the yielding throng.

Weaponed well, to war we ride ;
The ball is open, the hall is wide —
The sabre, as it quits the sheath,
And beams with the lurid light of death,
    And the deadly glance
    Of the glittering lance,
Are the taper-lights of the battle-dance.

Weaponed well, to war we ride —
Find your foemen on either side,
But woe to those who miss the time,

Where one false step is a deadly crime;
    Who loses breath,
    In the dance of death,
Wins, nor wears, nor wants the wreath.

Weaponed well, to war we ride —
Our swords are keen, our cause is tried;
When the keen edge cuts and the blood runs free,
May we die in the hour of victory!
    We feel no dread;
    The battle-bed,
Where'er it be, has heaven o'erhead.

———◆———

SONG OF THE NEW HAMPSHIRE VOLUNTEERS

BY MARIAN DOUGLAS.

DEDICATED TO THE SEVENTH NEW HAMPSHIRE REGIMENT.

FROM hill-top and mountain
    We press to the fight;
Up, up with our banner,
    For God and the Right!
We dare not stay weakly
    And trembling at home;

The moment for action,
    For conflict, has come!
Chorus — The fire sweeps the prairie,
        The tempest the sea,
    But nothing can conquer
        The hearts of the free!

'T is ours to keep burning,
    On hill-top and glade,
The fire on the altars
    Our fathers have made.
Our hearts beat together,
    And shall to the last;
Who fears for the future,
    That thinks of the past?
        The fire sweeps, &c.

Then up with the banner!
    Mid sunlight or shade,
Before we would suffer
    Its brightness to fade,
Amid the wild tumult
    Upon the red plain,
Our hearts, with their life-blood,
    Would die it again!
        The fire sweeps, &c.

A NEGRO-VOLUNTEER SONG.

Air — "*Hoist up the Flag.*"

This song was written by a private in Company A, Fifty-Fourth (colored) Regiment, Massachusetts Volunteers.

FREMONT told them when the war it first
 begun,
How to save the Union, and the way it should be
 done ;
But Kentucky swore so hard, and old Abe he had
 his fears,
Till every hope was lost but the colored volunteers ;
Chorus — O, give us a flag, all free without a slave ;
We'll fight to defend it as our fathers did so brave ;
The gallant Comp'ny " A " will make the Rebels
 dance,
And we'll stand by the Union if we only have a
 chance.

McClellan went to Richmond with two hundred
 thousand brave ;
He said " keep back the niggers," and the Union
 he would save.

Little Mac he had his way, still the Union is in
  tears,
Now they call for the help of the colored volunteers.
          O, give us a flag, &c.

Old Jeff. says he 'll hang us if we dare to meet him
  armed, —
A very big thing, but we are not at all alarmed, —
For he first has got to catch us, before the way is
  clear,
And "that is what 's the matter" with the colored
  volunteer.
          O, give us a flag, &c.

So rally, boys, rally, let us never mind the past.
We had a hard road to travel, but our day is
  coming fast ;
For God is for the Right, and we have no need to
  fear ;
The Union must be saved by the colored volunteer.
          O, give us a flag, &c.

A SONG FOR THE TIME.

AIR — "*The Old English Gentleman.*"

COME, listen to another song,
  That shall make your heart beat high,
Bring the crimson to your forehead,
  And the lustre to your eye.
A song of the days of old,
  Of the years that have long gone by,
And of the yeomen, stout and bold,
  As ere wore sword on thigh.
    Of the brave old Yankee yeomen,
    Of the days of Seventy-six.

For when the news was spread abroad,
  The struggle had begun,
Far over all our Northern hills
  They started up as one;
And from many a farm and workshop,
  Ere the setting of the sun,
They water'd with their sacred blood
  The field of Lexington.
    The true old Yankee yeomen,
    Of the days of Seventy-six!

They were the first to bend the knee,
  When the standard waved abroad,
They were the first to face the foe
  On Bunker's bloody sod;
And ever in the van of fight,
  The foremost, still, they trod,
Until on many a well-fought field,
  They gave their souls to God.
    Like true old Christian yeomen,
    The men of Seventy-six!

And now their sons all rise again,
  With hearts as brave and true —
The good old times are gone, and yet,
  Thank God! we have these new;
The tree our sires had planted
  Seemed withering where it grew,
But now, 't is bursting into bloom
  'Neath heaven's own light and dew.
    The glorious Tree of Liberty,
    The seed of Seventy-six!

THE NORTHMEN ARE COMING.

BY GEORGE PERRY.

THE Northmen are coming, Oho! oho!
   The Northmen are coming, Oho! oho!
   The Northmen, the Northmen,
   The warriors of Freedom!
The Northmen are coming, Oho! oho!

Their star-spangled banners I see, I see!
The plume-crested horsemen I see, I see!   [ing,
   Down mountain and valley the hosts are stream-
And shouting the battle-cry, " One and Free."
      The Northmen are coming, &c.

The peal of their bugles I hear, I hear!
The clangor of trumpets I hear, I hear!
   The banners outflame the blazing morn,
O'er billows of bayonet, sword, and spear.
      The Northmen are coming, &c.

With rattle of musket, they come, they come!
With thunder of cannon, they come, they come!
   With tempest of fire, and storm of steel,
To drive out the traitors from Freedom's home.
      The Northmen are coming, &c.

The boom of their cannon is Tyranny's knell ;
Wherever they battle shall Liberty dwell ;
    They fight for the holiest hope of man,
They triumph with Washington, Bruce, and Tell.
    The Northmen are coming, &c.

They come with the banners our sires unfurled,
Unfurled for the exile, the bondman, the world,
    And Heaven shall speed their victorious march,
Till Liberty's foes to the dust be hurled.
    The Northmen are coming, &c.

UNION SONG.

INSCRIBED TO COLONEL CROOKS'S REGIMENT,

BY W. H. C. HOSMER.

WHEN our fathers in vain sought redress from
      the throne,
  And the tyrant grew mad in his thirst for domin-
    ion,
Earth shook while the bugle of conflict was blown,
  And our eagle unfolded his newly-fledged pinion ;
    Men with hair thin and white,
    Bared their arms for the fight,

And the lad of sixteen made the dull weapon bright;
  While, guiding the battle-storm, rolling in wrath,
  The star-flag of Freedom streamed full in their
        path.

The bird to that banner forever allied,
  Was born in the cloud, and baptized by the
        thunder;
And deeply in blood will his talons be dyed,
  Ere its clustering stars shall be riven asunder;
      And fiercely their light,
      Through the smoke of the fight,
Shall flash, making traitors grow pale at the sight;
  And the sun, overtaken by death, shall grow
        cold,
  When the banner we hail is no longer unrolled.

Black Treason shall never put foot on the flag
  That floated the blast when Cornwallis was taken;
And ere it give place to a Palmetto rag,
  The dead on the field of their fame will awaken;
      Oh, shall it be furled,
      Bringing night on the world,
While the house of our fathers in ruin is hurled?
  The brigand and traitor may hear a reply
  In the clash of our steel and the rallying cry !

Our bold Harry Clay loved this land of the free,
  His name from Old Jackson we will not dissever,
Then spliced be your Ash to the Hickory-tree,
  And let them be symbols of Union forever;
      Without fear in their hearts,
      Well they acted their parts,
Though traitors showered on them their deadliest
        darts;
  And true to their Maker and faithful to man,
  The standard of Freedom they bore in the van.

From the North to the Tropic shall float on the
      gale
  Our star-flag, upheld by the brave and the just;
Though a wretched Disunion banditti assail,
  They shall not drag down its proud eagle to dust.
      Then arm for the strife,
      Give them war to the knife,
And light in the balance with Union bold life;
  Our flag to the breeze that a Washington blest,
  Though torn, must wave over Charleston again.

16

THE "OLD CONCERN."

A NEW SONG, BY UNCLE SAM.

THE " Old Concern," which has so long
    Its banner bright unfurled —
In honor, truth, and glory strong —
    The pride of all the world !
Ah ! cowards, if one spark of shame
    Can in your bosom burn,
Reflect how much you owe the name
    Of that good " Old Concern."

Through long, long years, your happy lot
    It made for you ; and then
It gave — what else you ne'er had got —
    A station among men ;
Without its aid which of you, pray,
    An honest cent would earn ?
And yet you wish to run away,
    And leave the " Old Concern."

Remember Bunker ! Lexington !
    The Delaware ! Yorktown !
Fields where our fathers fought and won
    Their glory and renown !

To Vernon go, and thoughtfully
   Gaze on yon sacred urn,
Then think what caitiffs you must be,
   To curse the " Old Concern ! "

You 're rich, because you robbed my till,
   And cotton makes you great ;
You 'd shut up shop against my will,
   But cotton you can't eat ;
And when your negroes run away,
   You then, perhaps, will learn
It had been wiser far to stay,
   And mind the " Old Concern."

When anarchy's dread wings unfurl
   Upon that shore so dark,
To which ambitious fiends would hurl
   Your frail and happy bark,
Ah ! then, perhaps — but when too late —
   You 'll hopelessly discern,
How happier was your former state
   When in the " Old Concern."

O madmen ! time will surely come
   When you, in grief, will learn
To taste again the sweets of home,
   Within the " Old Concern."

Ah! yes, you 'll come before not long,
  In penitent return,
To strive and wipe out all the wrong
  You 've done the " Old Concern ! "

---◆---

SONG OF THE VOLUNTEERS.

Tune—"*Marching Along.*"

AROUSE for the conflict ; why linger ye here ?
  Away, while the summons still rings on the
    ear, —
Away to the thousands of hearts, brave and strong,
And join in the ranks while they are marching
    along.
  Marching along, we are marching along,
  Union and Liberty shall still be our song,
  For Union we battle, and our blows true and
    strong,
  We strike for our Union while we are marching
    along.

The tramp of the steed and the roll of the drum,
Proclaim the glad answer — " We surely will
    come ; "

From hill-top and valley are pouring the throng,
To join in the battle they are marching along.
　Marching along, &c.

Oh! ye who have slumbered so long at your ease,
And dreamed in your quiet homes visions of peace,
Arouse from your slumber, and crush out the wrong,
And join in our army now marching along.
　Marching along, &c.

Awake to the glory, awake in your might,
Ye sons of the heroes who conquered in fight
The proud Queen of Ocean, so vain and so strong,
Who scorns our brave troops that are marching
　　along.
　Marching along, &c.

Awake to the peril that threatens our land,
Arm, arm for the conflict, and with the keen brand
Give blows to the traitor, both heavy and strong,
And join our brave band that is marching along.
　Marching along, &c.

In vain shall the flag of the Rebel uprear,
We'll crush the vile emblem of pride and of fear,
And raise our own banner, with shouting and song,
And bear it aloft while marching along.
　Marching along, &c.

GOD SAVE THE GRAND OLD STARS AND STRIPES.

GOD of our fathers, bless the land
  We hold from them and thee ;
Stretch forth through rolling years the hand
  That made to keep us free.
In the world's onward march, grant Thou,
  Our nation lead the van,
Foremost in right and righteousness,
  In love to God and man.

Chorus :

  God keep these States United States,
    One nation of the free,
  God save the grand old Stars and Stripes,
    Of blood-bought liberty.

Like some great temple, arched and domed
  And many-columned, rise,
Sacred as very house of God,
  Thou Union, to the skies.
As thine own rugged, rock-bound coasts
  Resist the ocean's rage,
Stand thou 'gainst earth's embattled hosts,
  Unmoved from age to age.

  God keep these States,. &c.

Firm as the earth's foundations rest
  The pillars of our State,
Based on those virtues which alone
  Make men and nations great.
· So shall that sacred bond sublime,
  Which binds our States in one,
Resist the stormy shock of time,
  And stand while shines the sun.
      God keep these States, &c.

IOWA SOLDIERS.

BY S. SKEMP.

ASK me the song I wish to sing;
  'T is that which made the Union ring,
When Victory's song arose and burst
In thunders from the Iowa First,
      At Wilson's Creek.

The key-note struck, the music roll'd,
Where'er the flag the stars unfold;
Above the flag, above the stars,
The song arose above old Mars,
      Thanks to Belmont.

Lo ! Freedom's song rolls onward still,
The nation sings it with a will ;
The battle's fought, the victory's won,
Sung by the Twelfth at Donelson,
    And Iowa Second.

Hark ! from the west the warlike shout
In wild harmonious strains rings out,
From Pea Ridge comes the thrilling cry —
We 've fought the foe and made him fly !
    Brave Iowa boys.

Through the land, on ev'ry sea,
The battle-song of victory,
Begun by Iowa's noble men,
Shall finish with their loud Amen,
    The Union's safe !

———◆———

SONG FOR BATTLE.

AIR — "*Marseillaise.*"

I.

OH comrades, going forth to battle,
    Forget to doubt — forget to fear ;
And when the balls around us rattle,
    Let step be firm, and eye be clear.

See how the foeman's lines are swaying,
 See how they waver left and right:
Charge on, our captain's voice obeying,
 And put their breaking ranks to flight !
Chorus — Arise, arise, ye brave,
    And take your swords in hand ;
    March on, march on, resolved to sav ?
    Our Union and our land !

II.

See where our sacred flag is flying,
 Each star and every stripe is there ;
Oh, swear to guard it well, relying
 Upon the cause that bids us swear.
It guards us well on land and water,
 And speaks a mighty Union's praise ;
Defend it now 'mid smoke and slaughter,
 Where bay'nets stab and muskets blaze.
   Arise, arise, ye brave, &c.

III.

But is the strife of our beginning ?
 And do we thirst for Southern blood ?
Oh, no; when traitors cease from sinning
 We 'll clasp the South in brotherhood.
Though now the battle-shouts are ringing,
 And anger flames from every eye,

Yet are ye safe who join our singing,
  " The Union — it shall never die ! "
    Arise, arise, ye brave, &c.

C. B.

DIXIE.

BY T. M. COOLEY.

A WAY down South, where grows the cotton,
  'Seventy-six seems quite forgotten ;
    Far away, far away, far away, Dixie land.
And men, with Rebel shout and thunder,
Tear our good old flag asunder,
    Far away, far away, far away, Dixie land.
Then we 're bound for the land of Dixie !
      Hurrah ! hurrah !
In Dixie land we 'll take our stand,
  And plant our flag in Dixie !
Away, away, away down South in Dixie !
Away, away, away down South in Dixie !

That flag — the foemen quailed before it,
When our patriot-fathers bore it,
  Far away, &c.
And battle-fields are shrined in story,
Where its folds were bathed in glory,
  Far away, &c.

And now, when traitor-hands assail it,
Stanch defenders ne'er shall fail it ; —
    Far away, &c.
Nor from its glorious constellation
Stars be plucked by pirate nation ; —
    Far away, &c.

Undimmed shall float that starry banner,
Over Charleston and Savannah,
    Far away, &c.
And Bunker Hill and Pensacola
Own alike its mission holy ; —
    Far away, &c.

Then sound the march ! We pledge devotion
In our blood on land or ocean,
    Far away, &c.
Till every traitor in the nation
Gains a Haman's elevation,
    Far away, &c.

Yes, sound the march ! Our Northern freemen
Turn not back for man or demon,
    Far away, far away, far away, Dixie land.
Until once more our banner, glorious,
Waves over Dixie land victorious,
    Far away, far away, far away, Dixie land.

TO THE TENTH LEGION,*

That passed down Broadway singing the Refrain,

"FOR GOD AND OUR COUNTRY, WE ARE MARCHING ALONG."

BY RUTH N. CROMWELL.

MARCHING along! — marching to the war —
    I saw them as they passed, a thousand men
      or more;
Their bayonets were gleaming in the sun's burning
    light,
For God and their Country, they were marching
    to the fight, —
    Marching along — marching along —
"For God and our Country, we are marching
    along."

I could not see their banners, for my eyes grew
    dim;
I but thought of my country, and sublime grew
    their hymn,
Till my soul echoed back, oh! again and again,
The song of the battle! — the soldiers' refrain —

* New York State Volunteers.

Marching along — marching along —
"For God and our Country, we are marching
  . along."

I have bowed to the song, when love was the
    theme ;
I have listened to the chime, when fame was the
    dream ;
Not the psalmodies of life, nor the cadences of
    art,
Were so grand to my ear, or so dear to my
    heart —
    Marching along — marching along —
"For God and our Country, we are marching
    along."

Loud blew the bugle — God keep them where
    they roam,
For the hearts that are waiting, for the firesides at
    home —
Loud blew the bugle, and they answered in their
    might,
For God and our Country, we are marching to the
    fight.
    Marching along — marching along —
"For God and our Country, we are marching
    along."

Marching along — marching along —
Brave were their hearts, and brave was their song.
O, I know there are leaves on the old bay-tree,
That are growing for their brows, in the land of
     the free, —
    Marching along — marching along —
" For God and their Country, they were marching
     along."

A RECRUITING RALLY.

BY " PORTLAND."

MEN of Maine ! men of Maine !
    Now again, now again,
Our country calls her sons to the field :
    Leave your work, leave your plough,
    Rally prompt, rally now,
For *Dirigo* 's emblazed on Maine's shield.

    Hold not back, hold not back,
    Glory's track, glory's track
Opes to us, as it did to our sires ;
    What they built, we renew,
    Let their sons light anew
Freedom's pure flame, of Liberty's fires.

As our pine, as our pine,
Always shine, always shine,
'Ever verdant, amid winter's blast ;
Let our faith in the Right
Make us stand to the fight,
Not relax while the battle doth last.

Sons of Maine ! Sons of Maine !
Not in vain, not in vain,
Let our brothers encamped call for aid ;
Let the Seven Thousand* charge !
With the ONE-ARMED, at their targe,
And Rebellion at our feet will be laid.

THE SONS OF OLD LUZERNE.

BY M. L. T. HARTMAN.

ALL honor to our Luzerne boys,
    Who volunteered to save our land !
Who left kind friends and fireside joys,
    To join the patriotic band.

When Freedom's blast was issued forth
From our Republic's capitol,

* Maine's quota of 300,000.

And woke the millions of the North,
  To answer to their country's call —

Then Luzerne's noble sons it found,
  Immersed in trade; in works of skill;
In the deep mines; in lore profound;
  In pleading law, for others' will;

In farming, too, were many more,
  Each busy in his peaceful home,
Who ne'er had taken thought before,
  That soldier he should e'er become.

But when our country, in her need,
  Proclaimed that Treason must be crushed,
The Luzerne patriot-sons gave heed,
  And forth, to offer help, they rushed.

Each branch of trade sent forth her men,
  Our Laws and Liberties to save;
Merchants and miners, equal then,
  Ploughmen and printers, all were brave.

The lawyer left his client's cause;
  The student laid his book aside;
Mechanics, to support our laws,
  Went forth in honest, patriot pride.

Mothers and sisters said " Good-by,"
　And bade them ne'er to treason bend;
And wives, though with a tearful eye,
　Said, " Go, our Union's flag defend."

Our noble braves we love and bless;
　We think of them with glowing pride;
Their valor will insure success;
　Their virtues, pure, will e'er abide.

God bless and save our Luzerne boys!
　Keep them when on the tented field;
Grant them the purest of all joys;
　In battle's roar from danger shield.

WILKESBARRE, Pa., *July* 3, 1861.

———◆———

"FAUGH A BALLAUGH."

WAR-SONG FOR THE IRISH BRIGADE.

BEHOLD the banner of the brave,
　Crowned with that glorious constellation —
Oh! may it long triumphant wave,
　The hope of every struggling nation;
Let dastard traitors do their worst,
　That emblem of our country's valor

Shall not be trampled in the dust —
   Up, sons of Ireland ! — " Faugh a ballaugh. " *

Shall villains drag our starry flag,
   By the blood of warriors consecrated,
And raise instead that viper's head †
   O'er Northern freemen subjugated ?
No, no ; the boasts of Southern hosts,
   By Heaven ! right soon we 'll make them swallow :
They 'll shortly feel our Yankee steel,
   Backed by an Irish " Faugh a ballaugh."

O 'er many a battle-field of yore
   That wild war-slogan hath resounded ;
From famed Cremona to Lahore,
   Still twining wreaths of laurel round it,
At Fontenoy it swept away,
   Whilst vengeance in its track did follow,
Till the Saxon legions of Lord Hay
   Went down before that " Faugh a ballaugh."

From Mantua's walls unto the Seine,
   With victory perched upon their banner,
The children of our crownless queen
   Won fortune, title, rank, and honor.

* Clear the way.   † The rattlesnake.

We go to emulate their fame —
  Here Freedom o'er us sheds its halo:
Our battle-cry is still the same —
  Brave sons of Erin, " Faugh a ballaugh."

We guard the banner of the free,
  ·Crowned with a glorious constellation —
The heaven-born flag of liberty,
  And hope of every struggling nation.
Let dastard traitors do their worst,
  That emblem of our country's valor
Shall not be trampled in the dust; —
  Up, sons of Ireland ! — " Faugh a ballaugh."

———◆———

STEP TO THE FRONT, SONS OF THE HEATHER.

DEDICATED TO THE HIGHLAND GUARD, SEVENTY-NINTH REGIMENT,
N. Y. S. M.

STEP to the front, bonnet and feather,
  Linked with the dreams of your own Highland
    vale ;
Step to the front, sons of the heather,
  Show the bold Southrons the face of the Gael.

The lords of the South have unkennelled their
    beagles,
  The legions of tyranny sweep from afar;
We welcome you, lads, to the feast of the eagles,
  The van of the battle — the honors of war.
        Step to the front, bonnet and feather, &c.

Flowers of the vale they have crushed down before
    them;
  All to the will of the despots must bow;
But manhood has met them, and death hovers o'er
    them —
  The strong-bearded thistle is waiting them now.
        Step to the front, bonnet and feather, &c.

Down on them, Highlanders, swoop from your eyry,
  Ruffle the tartans, and give the claymore;
Read them a lesson to pause and to fear ye
  When gathered the rights of the free to restore.
        Step to the front, bonnet and feather, &c.

THE GALLANT TENTH.*

BY WILLIAM H. DAVIE.

DASH on ! dash on ! our gallant Tenth !
  Where dangers darkly frown ;
Let Freedom bravely nerve our arms,
  Strike every traitor down !
What though their murd'rous squadrons stand
  In stern and fierce array,
We 'll make them feel our sweeping charge,
  And quickly clear the way.

This Union, which so long has been
  The sheltering-place for all
Fair Freedom's valiant, holy band,
  Shall not by traitors fall ;
But it will stand through storm and strife,
  The beacon of all lands ;
And naught shall cause its overthrow,
  While strength lies in our hands.

Our courage is of parent-blood,
  And why should we stay back,
While we have in our gallant band
  The men that never lack.

* Tenth Regiment, Michigan Infantry.

Our bold commander, Colonel Lum,
  Who has bravely faced our foes,
Is now resolved to strike again, —
  Strike heavy, stalwart blows.

Our gallant little company
  Of Union men alone,
Are bound to stand up by the flag,
  As long as there is one.
So come on, our true Captain!
  Lead to the charge along;
And see what your brave men can do
  With that rebellious gang.

Though years may roll their onward course,
  Our hands shall ne'er be stayed,
Till Freedom's land is free from strife,
  And in sweet peace arrayed.
And now, farewell to home and friends,
  And if we ne'er return,
'T will be because the gallant Tenth
  All death and danger spurn.

UNION SONG OF THE CELT.

BY WILLIAM E. ROBINSON.

HAIL! brightest banner that floats on the gale!
Flag of the country of Washington, hail!
Red are thy stripes with the blood of the brave,
Bright are thy stars as the sun on the wave;
Wrapt in thy folds are the hopes of the free;
Banner of Washington! blessings on thee!

Mountain-tops mingle the sky with their snow;
Prairies lie smiling in sunshine below;
Rivers, as broad as the sea, in their pride,
Border thine empires, but do not *divide;*
Niagara's voice far out-anthems the sea;
Land of sublimity! blessings on thee!

Hope of the world! on thy mission sublime,
When thou didst burst on the pathway of Time,
Millions from darkness and bondage awoke;
Music was born when Liberty spoke;
Millions to come shall yet join in the glee;
Land of the pilgrim's hope! blessings on thee!

Traitors shall perish, and treason shall fail;
Kingdoms and thrones in thy glory grow pale!

Thou shalt live on, and thy people shall own
Loyalty 's sweet, where each heart is thy throne,
Union and Freedom thine heritage be, —
Country of Washington ! blessings on thee !

THE GALLANT BOYS OF KEYES' BRIGADE.

BY DR. REYNOLDS,

Assistant-Surgeon Twenty-fourth Regiment, N. Y. S. V.

WE 'RE ready all to meet the foe,
    With hearts resolved and spirits gay ;
And every brow wears the bright glow
    Of glory from the coming fray.
We have too long been waiting here ;
    And now, at last, in arms arrayed,
We 're moving onward with a cheer —
    The gallant boys of Keyes' Brigade.

They 're coming on ! Won't it be sport ?
    They 'll not have very far to come ;
For we will make their journey short,
    And meet them more than half way home.
And when we meet, oh, won't they pray
    That they afar from us had stayed,
And had not dared, upon this day,
    The gallant boys of Keyes' Brigade.

We dearly love our native land,
  The land of liberty and fame,
And never will our patriot-band
  To her bring injury or shame.
Oh, never yet did lover glow
  To meet his bride, in smiles arrayed,
As do, to meet the pursuing foe,
  The gallant boys of Keyes' Brigade.

The Brooklyn boys, the lads of Troy,
  Oswego's strong, heroic band,
And Albany's, with souls of joy,
  In one unwavering phalanx stand.
We move to meet the Rebel host,
  United, gay, and undismayed—
Come, traitors, on! o'er you will boast
  The gallant boys of Keyes' Brigade.

If death should come, why let it come;
  Death is more welcome than defeat;
To die for liberty and home
  Is death most glorious and most sweet.
Let us but see, with fading eye,
  Our banner float o'er foes low laid,
And death we 'll greet with victory,
  The gallant boys of Keyes' Brigade.

SONG.

AIR — "*Scots wha ha' wi' Wallace bled.*"

FREEMEN of the hardy North
   Pour your banded thousands forth,
For your country's cause is worth
    All your energies.
Traitors leagued betray her right,
Rebels dare defy her might,
Up ! and blast their traitorous spite,
    Gallant Northmen, rise !

Men who conquered at Champlain,
Chippewa, and Lundy's Lane,
Live to lead your hosts again
    On to victory.
Shall the Great Republic fail ?
Shall her star-decked banner quail,
Rent and shattered in the gale
    Of rampant slavery ?

Never, while Niagara's deep
Pours its torrent down the steep,
And the crystal mountains keep
    Pointing up to heaven.

Comrades of the hardy North,
Ye have rushed by thousands forth ;
Emulate your fathers' worth,
    Strive as they have striven.

                      T. B.

THE FOURTH NEW JERSEY VOLUNTEERS.

BY JOHN G. DORAN.

TUNE — "*Plains of Mexico.*"

ATTENTION give, brave volunteers,
  New-Jersey Fourth, I mean,
To-day you 're in the army here,
  To view uncommon scenes.

You have left your homes and families,
  And enlisted in the cause,
To join the Union army,
  And protect our country's laws.

All things are nearly ready,
  And we soon expect to meet
Those Rebels who have trampled
  Our flag beneath their feet.

Then when, amid the cannon's roar,
 The heavy blows you strike
For Union and for Liberty,
 God will protect the Right.

But should you in the conflict fall,
 When Victory is the cry,
I know it will be facing them —
 A soldier's death you 'll die.

Cheer up, cheer up, brave volunteers,
 Whate'er our fate may be,
We 'll stand up for that noble flag,
 Our homes and liberty.

A name you bear, brave Jersey Fourth,
 No other can excel,
And when you to the conflict go,
 Your actions there will tell

That Jersey blood is in us still,
 And like a tide will rise,
Whenever traitors trample on
 The flag we dearly prize.

Jerseymen, remember still,
 Our fathers with gray hair

Fought at Monmouth and at Trenton,
   And crossed the Delaware.

With bloody feet they made their marks,
   Our liberty to gain ;
New-Jersey Fourth, the time may come
   For us to do the same.

And when this conflict 's at an end,
   Shall stop the cannon's noise,
I ever shall remember well
   The Fourth New-Jersey boys.

Oh ! yes, our cause must surely win,
   That flag must float as free —
Six hundred thousand volunteers
   Shall gain the victory.

So now farewell, brave volunteers,
   Till on the field we meet ;
May heaven bless each Jerseyman,
   Who never knows defeat.

THE STRIPES AND STARS.

BY EDNA DEAN PROCTOR.

AIR — " *The Star-Spangled Banner.*"

OH, Star-Spangled Banner! the flag of our
    pride !
Though trampled by traitors and basely defied,
Fling out to the glad winds, your red, white and
    blue,
For the heart of the Northland is beating for you !
And her strong arm is nerving to strike with a will,
Till the foe and his boastings are humbled and still !
Here 's welcome to wounding, and combat, and
    scars,
And the glory of death — for the Stripes and the
    Stars !

From prairie, O ploughman ! speed boldly away —
There 's seed to be sown in God's furrows to-day —
Row landward, lone fisher ! stout woodman, come
    home !
Let smith leave his anvil and weaver his loom,
And hamlet and city ring loud with the cry,
" For God and our Country we 'll fight till we die !
Here 's welcome to wounding, and combat, and scars,
And the glory of death — for the Stripes and the
    Stars ! "

Invincible Banner ! the Flag of the Free !
O where treads the foot that would falter for thee ?
Or the hands to be folded, till triumph is won
And the eagle looks proud, as of old, to the sun ?
Give tears for the parting — a murmur of prayer —
Then forward ! the fame of our standard to share !
With welcome to wounding, and combat, and scars,
And the glory of death — for the Stripes and the
    Stars.

———◆——

LITTLE CROW.

SUNG BY COMPANY A, SIXTH REGIMENT, MINNESOTA VOLUNTEERS.

COME, all you young fellows,
    Who have a mind to range
Into some Indian country,
    Your fortunes to change ;
All for the love of pleasure,
    We wander to and fro ;
With our scouts out on the prairie.
Chorus — We 'll chase Little Crow ;
        We 'll chase Little Crow ;
        With our scouts out on the prairie,
        We will chase Little Crow.

There are fishes in the river,
  All fitting for our use ;
And fine lofty sugar-canes
  Will yield to us their juice ;
There are all sorts of game, my boys,
  Besides the buck and doe ;
With our scouts out on the prairie,
    We'll chase Little Crow.
    We'll chase, &c.

Come, all you pretty, fair maidens,
  And spin us some yarn,
That we may have some clothing,
  To keep ourselves warm ;
O you may card and spin, sweet girls,
  While we pursue the foe ;
With our scouts out on the prairie,
    We'll chase Little Crow.
    We'll chase, &c.

Supposing those wild Indians
  By chance should interfere,
We'll all unite together,
  With our hearts free from care ;
We'll march into their tepees,
  And strike the deadly blow ;

With our scouts out on the prairie,
   We 'll chase Little Crow.
   We 'll chase, &c.

And if by chance we get his scalp,
   We 'll take it neat and clean ;
It will be the nicest trophy
   We ever yet have seen,
For with good aim we shoot our game,
   In revenge for those who fell ;
And with our minie bullets
   We 'll send his soul to ——.
   We 'll chase, &c.

Here 's a health to our comrades,
   And our gallant Colonel Crooks ;
He is a good leader,
   We know him by his looks ;
And when the war is ended,
   And homeward bound we go,
We will pass the sparkling glass,
   And talk of Little Crow.
   We 'll chase, &c.

THE ARMY TO THE PEOPLE.

BY CAROLINE A. MASON.

MEN of the North! ye are true, ye are strong!
  Give us a watchword to cheer us along;
Write on our banners, in letters of fire,
Words that shall hearten, enoble, inspire;
Words that shall strike to the heart of the foe
Terror and trembling wherever we go;
Give us *this* watchword to bear through the fight:
" Freedom and Fatherland, God and the Right!"

" Freedom " for all who are weak and oppressed —
" Fatherland, God, and the Right!" For the rest,
Leave that to us! With a watchword so true,
What shall be lacking that brave hearts can do?
Soon, from the Gulf to the border, o'er moat,
O'er battlement, fortress, that banner should float,
Blazoned all over with letters of light:
" Freedom and Fatherland, God and the Right!"

Men of the North! ye are firm, ye are leal!
Firmer than granite and truer than steel!
Loving and loyal, this only remains:
Strike from the bondman his fetters and chains!

Then, *then* shall our legions go forth to the fray,
Invincible, clad in their battle-array;
And conquering angels shall lead on the fight
For Freedom and Fatherland, God and the Right!

VETERAN SONG OF THOMAS' OLD CORPS.

BY "DELTA."

HAVE our hearts grown colder, comrades?
  Is our country's flag less dear?
Though our thoughts may wander homewards,
  Can we leave the Old Flag here?
While our thinn'd ranks front the foemen
  We so oft have met before,
Who would cheer us, man or woman,
  Should we leave the brave old Corps?

By the star-lit folds above us —
  By our comrades mould'ring low —
By the hopes of those who love us —
  We will turn not from the foe!
While our thinn'd ranks front the foemen
  We so oft have met before,
Who would cheer us, man or woman,
  Should we leave the brave old Corps?

Peace may come and we may greet it —
  If we should not, be it so —
Death or danger, let us meet it,
  Giving more than blow for blow !
While our thinn'd ranks front the foemen
  We so oft have met before,
Who would cheer us, man or woman,
  Should we leave the brave old Corps ?

Righteous battles we are fighting
  For our country — for her laws ;
Many odious wrongs are righting ;
  God is with us — with our cause !
While our thinn'd ranks front the foemen
  We so oft have met before,
Who would cheer us, man or woman,
  Should we leave the brave old Corps ?

TO THE GIRL I LEFT BEHIND.

BY A. VAN DYKE,

OF COMPANY E, FIRST MICHIGAN INFANTRY.

AIR — "*Bonny Doon.*"

DEAR friend, I sit me down to write
　　The thoughts, the feelings of my heart ;
Affection's fires are burning bright,
　　Affection's tear perchance may start,
For miles of distance now divide
　　The soldier from his friends at home,
But in thy heart I can confide,
　　Where'er on earth my footsteps roam.

Fond memory keeps her treasure well —
　　Thy sacred image still is there —
It cheers me like a magic spell,
　　And lightens many a weight of care.
That " parting scene " I'll ne'er forget —
　　The vows we pledged, the tears we shed —
Trust me they 're all.remembered yet,
　　Though many weary months have fled.

Though distant far from friends and home,
   Surrounded by the din of war,
The memories bright of friends behind
   Are still the soldier's guiding star ;
But should remembrance fail to trace
   The outlines of each cherished form,
The artist, with a magic grace,
   Portrays each feature " fresh and warm."

Dear friend, I thank you from my heart
   For that impression of your face,
'T will cheer me in some lonely hour,
   Each well-remembered mark to trace.
I 've placed it with my friends so dear,
   And guard them all with nicest care,
And when o'er theirs I shed a tear,
   Be sure that you 'll receive a share.

Blest be the artist's magic power,
   Thus brightly joining kindred hearts ;
'T is sunshine in the darkest hour,
   And firmer courage it imparts.
It cheers the soldier's lonely way,
   And brings contentment to his mind,
It brightens " love's undying ray,"
   And makes him to his lot resigned.

" Farewell, farewell, my far-off friend,
   Between us broad, blue rivers flow,
And forests wave, and plains extend,
   And mountains in the sunlight glow.
The breeze that blows upon thy brow
   Is not the breeze that blows on mine—
The moonbeams resting on thee now
   Are not the beams that on me shine."

And yet I trust we soon will meet,
   When war's dark clouds have passed away;
How pleasant then 't will be to greet
   The friends of life's bright morning day;
Our vows of love we 'll then renew,
   And swift the moments then will fly.
I will not speak "the cold adieu,"
   But now, my friend, " good-by, good-by."

FILL UP THE RANKS, BOYS.

BY L. S. W.

YES, fill up the ranks, boys,
   Of the brave " American Guards,"
And if you follow its colors well,
   From fights you ne'er will be debarred;

Our ranks are thinned by shot and shell,
  But still goes up our battle-cry :
Forward ! and charge upon the foe,
  For we 'll conquer or we 'll die !

Our country calls for stalwart men
  To rally for the coming fray ;
Oh ! hear that call, ye loyal ones,
  To the field of strife, away, away ;
Away from your cool and shady bowers,
  From mother dear, and loved one's side,
From friends you love, and social hours,
  To fill the place of those who 've died.

It bids you go and stand with those,
  Who battle for the cause of Right ;
With gleaming bayonets beat back the foe,
  Now marshalled for the coming fight ;
To bid them stay their wicked hands,
  Now red with friends' and brothers' gore ;
And seek again " their fathers' house,"
  In peace to live as in days before.

Oh ! is your country nothing worth
  That thus you idly stay at home,
In this her hour of greatest need,
  To see her perish, and alone ?

No ! yours be the honor now to raise
    Those " Stars and Stripes," so loved by all ;
And swear by Him who rules on high,
    By them to live or with them fall.

Then rally to our standard, boys, .
    Ye gallant ones and true ;
There is " Captain Jack " of Co. K,
    Who will gladly welcome you ;
We're going in the " Fortifications," boys ;
    These tidings sure will please ;
But mind it's not at Washington,
    But those of Rebel General Lee's.

CAMP, NEAR CULPEPPER, Va., *March* 12, 1864.

— ◆ —

AMERICA.

MY country, 't is of thee,
    Sweet land of liberty,
Of thee I sing :
Land where my fathers died,
Land of the Pilgrims' pride,
From every mountain-side,
    Let freedom ring.

My native country, thee,
Land of the noble, free —
    Thy name I love :
I love thy rocks and rills,
Thy woods and templed hills ;
My heart with rapture thrills,
    Like that above.

Let music swell the breeze,
And ring from all the trees,
    Sweet Freedom's song :
Let mortal tongues awake,
Let all that breathe partake,
Let rocks their silence break,
    The sound prolong.

Our fathers' God, to thee,
Author of liberty,
    To thee I sing :
Long may our land be bright
With Freedom's holy light ;
Protect us by thy might,
    Great God, our King.

SONG OF THE MARYLAND FIRST.

INSCRIBED TO COLONEL JOHN R. KENLY,

BY J. J. STEWART.

WE 'LL strike for our country,
Proud land of the Free !
Her banner floats o'er us,
And happy are we.
Its star-glistening quarter
Illumines the story
Of Liberty's triumphs
On red fields of glory !
Baptized in the blood of our fathers, we 'll cherish
And fight for our flag till the last man shall perish!
(Repeat.)

One blow for the Union
Though traitors assail
The bulwark of Freedom,
They cannot prevail.
Destruction awaits them —
The vengeance of Heaven !
Like chaff in the wild wind
Their hosts shall be driven !
Baptized in the blood of our fathers, we 'll cherish
And fight for the flag till our last man shall perish !

On, on, sons of Freedom !
The conscripts await
Your valorous charges
To settle their fate.
The despots that rule them
Shall flee from your power, —
The oppressed will rejoice in
The auspicious hour
That brings them the flag of their fathers — then
cherish
And fight for that flag till the last man shall perish !
Hurrah for the "Star-Spangled Banner," we'll
cherish
And fight for the flag till our last man shall perish !

———◆———

THE SONG OF OUR FLAG.

BY REV. H. HARBAUGH, D. D.

AIR — "*The Bells of Shandon.*"

WITH deep affection,
And recollection,
I often think of
Our glorious flag,
Whose folds so wild would
In days of childhood

Fling o'er my fancy
     Their magic spells.
See our flag yonder!
On that I ponder,
And still grow fonder,
     Proud flag, of thee.
Thy bright stars gleaming,
Thy broad stripes streaming,
In all my dreaming
     I seem to see.

I 've seen ovations
And jubilations,
To flags of nations,
     In every clime;
But the wild roaring
Of their adoring,
To me imploring,
     Had nought sublime.
For memory dwelling
On thy proud swelling,
With sweeter telling,
     Still spoke of thee —
Thy bright stars gleaming,
Thy broad stripes streaming,
In all my dreaming
     I seemed to see.

I 've seen flags, glorious,
Borne back victorious
From fields notorious
　　For blood and strife ;
For whose maintaining
The brave, disdaining
Dread missiles raining,
　　Gave up their life.
Of these flags, gory,
I 've heard the glory
In song and story,
　　Told tenderly ;
But thy stars gleaming,
Thy broad stripes streaming,
In all my dreaming
　　I ever see.

Devices olden,
With trimmings golden,
Seem to embolden,
　　The claims of these ;
Such empty tender
Of royal splendor
I all surrender,
　　With greatest ease.
See our flag yonder, —
On that I ponder,

And still grow fonder,
 Dear flag, of thee :
Thy bright stars gleaming,
Thy broad stripes streaming,
In all my dreaming
 I ever see.

Flag of our nation,
The best oblation
Of adoration
 I offer thee.
Tyrant and Tory
Have learned thy story —
The tale of glory
 And Liberty !
And children wondering,
And heroes pondering,
And cannon thundering,
 Shall honor thee !
Thy bright stars gleaming,
Thy broad stripes streaming,
In all my dreaming
 I ever see.

So runs the song of the old flag, true,
With thirty-four stars in its cloudless blue ;
Hiss that new burlesque — that treason-rag —
March to the tune of the good old flag.

THE GALLANT THIRTEENTH.*

Colonel Geary, in command at the battle of Bolivar
Heights, Va., said, " But for the Boston Company C, I
should have *lost* the day."

TRIED, and found not wanting! valiant, firm,
        and true,
Boston fathers' flowing hearts send greeting back
        to you;
Tears were dried in loving pride, when first you
        marched away,
How proudly now lifts every brow, that you have
        won the day !

They hear, they see your battle-field — not there
        th' impetuous shout,
Leads hastily, unwarily — then marks a Bull-Run
        rout;
But firm in stand as in resolve, they see you nobly
        dare,
And hold ! till Rebel foes, aghast, fly from your
        Bolivar !

* Massachusetts Volunteers.

Jackson, (propitious name,) lead on ! Centurion of
  the Free !
And, where an enemy appears, show him your
  Boston C ;
Their every volley echoes home — the Thirteenth
  is our boast,
And as we pledge to life and health, *that* number
  gems our toast !

Bravely you met the vaunting foe, bravely you
  have repelled,
Not counting platoons, but the *cause*, 'gainst which
  they have rebelled,
And victory crowns your first essay with her en-
  shrining wreath !
May it continue bloodless, when conq'ring swords
  you sheathe.

And now, all question put aside, they know you as
  you are,
The heroes who set odds at nought at *Heights of
  Bolivar !*
And *Harper's Ferry*, names which hence, long as
  Potomac roll,
Emblazoned, shine along the line, on the gallant
  Thirteenth's scroll !

F. V. B.

19

SONG OF THE SQUIRREL–HUNTER.

BY G. W. PETERS.

UP, arouse, my fellow-ranger,
   We are needed in the fray;
Our country is in danger;
   Seize your rifle and away.
Never shame your rig, old fellow,
   Other lads have shoddy suits,
Ours is baize and homespun yellow,
   Kossuth hat and hunter's boots.

Not a drum hath need to rattle,
   Not a bugle need be blown;
We are wanted in the battle,
   That is all that need be known.
Not a signal-gun at morning
   Speaks to call us to the war,
For we ask no other warning,
   Than our brother's cry from far.

Is the Rebel foe grown bolder?
   Does he come in armed array?
Not a star upon the shoulder
   Burns to light us on our way.

But we go to find and meet him,
  And the welcome we shall give,
When as man to man we greet him,
  Is, that ONLY ONE CAN LIVE.

Fled! and we may not pursue him —
  Back unto our homes again —
Oh! that we might go unto him!
  Hunt the tiger in his den.
We obey, for law and order
  Is our rule, as well as Right:
If again he nears our border,
  Call the hunters in their might.
CINCINNATI, Ohio, July, 1863.

———◆———

TRUMPET-SONG OF BATTLE.

TUNE —"*Here's a Health to King Charles.*"

COME, boys, join our song,
  Let it roll through the land,
We have loitered too long —
  Round our flag let us stand!
Be firm to your ground!
  Let your free banners wave,
While the trumpet shall sound,
  Here's a health to the brave!

Let the faint coward fly,
　　Now the battle 's begun ;
We will conquer or die,
　　But we never will run !
Stout hearts ! join our song,
　　For we fight but to save ;
Bring your banners along !
　　Here 's a health to the brave !

Oh, look ! how the light
　　Now streams o'er the land —
God's voice in the fight —
　　His arm leads our band !
Soon, the whole land around,
　　Our banner must wave,
While the trumpet shall sound
　　Here 's a health to the brave !

———◆———

THERE 'S A CORPS IN THE SERVICE.

Air — "*Boys of Kilkenny.*"

THERE 'S a corps in the service — the Bucktails
　　by name,
They 're the devils for fighting ; we belong to the
　　same ;

We care not for danger — we care not for wealth;
So fill up your glasses, and drink to our health.

We never were whipped — we never have run,
We fight not for bounty, — for our country we
    come,
To place the old flag on every mountain-top, —
So here 's our respects, will you take a wee drop ?

We 're the boys that are called on, when there 's
    work to be done,
And before the " Rebels " know it, we 'll whip five
    to one ;
Bullets don't scare us — we care not for noise ;
Come, empty your glasses, and drink to the boys.

Here 's a tear for our Colonel ; * he was one of the
    best ;
Here 's a sigh for the Bucktails that have gone to
    their rest ;
Glorious was their death — they fell fighting like
    men, —
Let us drink now in silence, in memory of them.

                     W. A. N.

   * Hugh W. McNeil, Colonel of the First Rifles, P. R. V.
C., killed at the battle of Antietam, Md., September 16,
1862.

WAR-SONG.

WRITTEN FOR THE FORTY-NINTH REGIMENT OF MASSACHUSETTS
VOLUNTEERS.

AIR — " *Columbia, the Gem of the Ocean.*"

OLD Berkshire, from hill and from valley,
    Her pride and her glory sends forth ;
Her brave sons unitedly rally,
    With the legions that pour from the North,
With firm will and manly endeavor,
    The Star-Spangled flag to uphold ;
Oh give us old Berkshire forever,
    And her own FORTY-NINTH, brave and bold !
Chorus — And her own Forty-Ninth, brave and bold.
        And her own Forty-Ninth, brave and bold.
        Oh give us old Berkshire forever,
        And her own Forty-Ninth, brave and bold.

We leave home and friends far behind us,
    And the scenes we have cherished so dear,
The ties that no longer must bind us,
    We sunder them all with a tear.
Ourselves from our kindred we sever,
    Till war and its perils are past ;
For the flag of our Union forever,
    We swear to defend to the last !
        We swear to defend to the last, &c.

By our Colonel, well skilled in commanding,
  Into battle we wait to be led ;
On a single sound leg he is standing,
  But he 's sound in his heart and his head.
At his bidding we 're going to follow,
  O'er the fields of the South far awa',
And we 'll vanquish the Rebels all hollow,
  Three cheers for our Colonel ! Hurra !
    Three cheers, &c.

Our Lieutenant-Colonel and Major —
  We know they are faithful and true ;
And victory's certain presager
  We hail in their courage to do.
At their lead, in right soldierly manner,
  The base Rebel-foe we 'll pursue ;
And we 'll tear down the secession banner,
  And fling out the Red, White, and Blue !
    And fling out, &c.

Our Captains are prompt to their duty,
  Lieutenants alert to each call ;
Our Staff boasts of valor and beauty ;
  And, in fact, we 're fine fellows all.
In Pittsfield, where we came together,
  In Worcester's generous town,

And even in Long Island weather,
  The old FORTY-NINTH takes 'em down !
  The old Forty-Ninth, &c.

Farewell to the homes we are leaving ;
  Farewell to the friends whom we know ;
Farewell to the lasses now grieving ;
  We 'll think of them all as we go.
For all these our hearts are yearning,
  While duty is beck'ning afar ;
And we 'll give, till God speeds our returning,
  Three cheers for sweet home ; Hip ! Hurra !
    Three cheers for sweet home ; Hip ! Hurra !
    Three cheers for sweet home ; Hip ! Hurra !
    And we'll give, till God speeds our returning,
    Three cheers for sweet home ; Hip ! Hurra !

———◆———

THE SOLDIER'S OATH.

BY REV. C. T. BROOKS.

LIFT on high both heart and hand !
  By the broad, blue heaven high o'er us,
  By the sacred cause before us,
Swear with Freedom's flag to stand !

By your forefathers in glory,
Names that consecrate the air,
  By your freedom's kindling story,
By the God of Freedom, swear!

Lift on high both heart and hand,
  Swear, that earth and heaven may hear it,
  And the brazen traitor fear it—
Swear the oath to save your land!
  Glorious ensign, float before us,
Proudly lead us to the field;
  While thy folds are fluttering o'er us,
None shall basely flee or yield!

Lift on high both heart and hand;
  Swell, with Freedom's pure air filling,
  Noble flag, each bosom thrilling
Of our chosen patriot-band;
  Sign of honor! never paling,
Save in death, our cheeks thou 'lt see —
  Thousand pangs with transport hailing,
Ere we turn our backs on thee!

Lift on high both heart and hand,
  Hail, this glorious consecration!
  Hail, regenerated nation!
Hail, all hail! thou new-born land!

Sons of Freedom, all assemble,
Solemn vows and praise to pay,
   Falsehood, fraud, and treason, tremble !
Courage, children of the day !

Lift on high both heart and hand,
   To the King of nations rear it,
   Let the great Heart-searcher hear it,
As we here before Him stand,
   Praying Him to keep us holy,
Pure in thought and word and deed —
   Him whose hand uplifts the lowly,
Makes the just alone succeed !

——◆——

WAR-SONG.

BY KANE O'DONNEL.

THE horse, for the valor of bounding,
   Is neighing with terrible breath,
The battle to glory is sounding,
   The trumpets are braying to death ;
But the hand of the warrior is steady,
The brand of the hero is ready.

Up, soul ! to thy dauntless delighting;
   Thy challenge the future has won,

Though the chasm be awful with lightning,
　Who fears not shall falter not.　On!
Strong heart! to thy summit bear proudly,
Did tempest shock never so loudly!

True spirit, wild, war-free! thine onward
　Advance is the errand of ruth,
And to cloudward, and starward, and sunward
　Career'st in the battle of Truth!
On! Freedom! fall, shackles, asunder,
And march to the roll of the thunder!

───◆───

SHOULDER ARMS.

BY C. G. DUNN.

THERE's a cry sweeps o'er the land —
　　Shoulder arms!
Who will now a coward stand,
While the country needs his aid?
Cowardice for fools was made.
　　Shoulder arms!

Who's afraid to meet the foe?
　　Shoulder arms!
Who would see the flag laid low

In the dust by traitors base !
Let him ever hide his face.
    Shoulder arms !

Who would win the soldier's fame ?
    Shoulder arms !
Who would bear a hero's name —
Let him raise his strong arms high,
Now to strike or now to die —
    Shoulder arms !

See the Rebel ranks advance :
    Shoulder arms !
Wake, man, from your guilty trance ;
This is time for action deep,
Not the hour for sloth or sleep !
    Shoulder arms !

Voices call you from the grave —
    Shoulder arms !
Voices of the martyrs brave,
Who, amid the shock of wars,
Battled for the Stripes and Stars.
    Shoulder arms !

By the names of heroes dead —
    Shoulder arms !

Precious hearts as yours have bled
To maintain the Union's might.
Now it is your turn to smite —
    Shoulder arms !

Onward! onward to the van —
    Shoulder arms !
Onward like a fearless man !
Stand not like one deaf and dumb,
While you hear th' appealing drum.
    Shoulder arms !

God will bless the work you do —
    Shoulder arms !
He will lead you safely through
Every peril, whilst you fight
" Gainst the Wrong," uphold the Right.
    Shoulder arms !

———◆———

MARCHING ON.

BY ESTELLE.

ANOTHER mighty army is gathering at the
    North !
Each loyal State is sending her many thousands
    forth !

They are rallying round the standard of our nation
    at her call,
And a fervent love of country nerves their spirits
    one and all,
        As they go marching on !

Their hearts have ne'er forgotten the voice that
    SUMTER spoke,
When its sounds in awful thunders on the startled
    nation broke ;
Its echoes still are lingering round the homes of
    Liberty,
And wake an answering chorus in the spirits of the
    free,
        As they go marching on !

Down in Virginia's valleys, where Potomac's waters
    glide,
Lies many a gallant soldier, who bravely fought and
    died !
A nation's love is circling, like a halo, where he
    lies !
While above are brightly arching the sunny south-
    ern skies.
        No more he marcheth on !

But 'mid far distant mountains full many a circle
    mourn

For fathers and for brothers, who will never more
       return !
For other hands than loving ones their resting-places
       made !
And stranger eyes are gazing on the spots where
       they were laid,
           When ceased their marching on !

Each soldier's heart is beating with a purpose firm
       and high —
As he thinks of this rebellion — to conquer it or
       die !
His cheeks are brightly glowing, and proudly flash
       his eyes,
Whene'er he thinks of Donelson's or Macon's vic-
       tories,
           As he goes marching on !

And when the thought comes o'er them how the
       noble LYON fell,
E'en to the last contesting for the cause he loved
       so well,
They sternly grasp their rifles and rush onward to
       the field ;
Resolved, that while life lasteth, they will never,
       never yield,
           But still go marching on !

Each brow is flushed with anger, when they think
    how ELLSWORTH died !
So young and noble was he ! our nation's pet and
    pride !
Yet *his* spirit was the *first* to leave this treason-
    tainted strand,
And put on heavenly armor in that bright, that
    better land,
        And there he marcheth on !

May God protect our brothers in the camp or in
    the field !
And be as He has promised, the soldier's strength
    and shield.
Be with them through the contest ! Return them
    to their friends !
And guide them to that city where pleasure never
    ends !
        There, ever to march on !

SONG OF THE BORDER.

AIR — " *Bonnie Dundee.* "

TO the heart of the nation the booming guns
    spoke,
While the true flag went down in the fire and the
    smoke ;
And the grim walls of Sumter yet echoed the fray,
When the Loyalists rushed where the Stars led the
    way.

Chorus — Then fight for the Stripes, boys, and fight
        for the Stars !
        Confounded be treason ! torn down be
           the Bars !
        Let foul traitors tremble, and Rebels
           grow pale,
        As the banner of the Union floats out
           on the gale !

Though the land of the cypress its vandals sends
    forth,
They are met in the path by the hosts of the North :
Toward the troopers that spring from the cotton-
    banked stream,
With the fires of just vengeance our bayonets
    gleam.
        Then fight, &c.
      20

They may flaunt in the breeze their famed rattle-
   snake flag;
They may sneer at the banner and call it a rag;
But by all we hold sacred, above or below,
We solemnly swear that their flag shall lie low! ·
        Then fight, etc.

They may boast of their chivalry, boast of their
   blood;
We stand by our fathers' faith, bow but to God:
Let them come in their pride; they shall griev-
   ously feel
The firmness and keenness of loyalists' steel.
        Then free let the Stripes wave, bright
           shine the Stars!
        Confounded be Treason! despised be
           the Bars!
        The false hearts of Rebels shall falter
           and quail,
        As the banner of Union floats out on
           the gale.

THE CAPTAIN OF '63 TO HIS MEN.

COME to the field, boys, come !
Come at the call of the stirring drum —
Come, boys, come !
Yonder 's the foe to our country's fame,
Waiting to blot out her very name —
Where is the man that would see her shame ?
Come, boys, come !

Form, my brave men, form !
Stand in order to " meet the storm "—
Form, men, form !
Sacred to us is our native land !
Shrivelled for aye be each traitor-hand
Lifted to shatter so bright a band —
Form, men, form !

Charge, my soldiers, charge !
From the steep hill to the river's marge,
Charge ! charge ! charge !
Think of our wives and mothers dear ;
Think of the hopes that have led us here ;
Think of the hearts that will give us cheer —
Charge, boys, charge !

Die with me, boys, die!
There's a place for all in yon bannered sky,
 If we die, boys, die!
Think of the names that are shining bright,
Written in letters of living light!
Rather than give up the sacred Right,
 Let's die, boys, die!

———◆———

OUR HOOSIER BOYS.

AIR — "*My Maryland.*"

DEDICATED TO THE SOLDIERS OF INDIANA.

FROM East to West your camp-fires blaze,
 Hoosier Boys! our Hoosier Boys!
On Vicksburg's heights our flag you raise,
 Hoosier Boys! our Hoosier Boys!
And on Virginia's trait'rous soil,
In answer to your country's call,
The echoes of your footsteps fall,
 Hoosier Boys! our Hoosier Boys!

While southern suns upon you beat,
 Hoosier Boys! our Hoosier Boys!

You sternly march the foe to meet,
    Hoosier Boys! our Hoosier Boys!
Two winters, numbered with the past,
    Have o'er you swept with stormy blast,
Since home's dear walls enclosed you last,
    Hoosier Boys! our Hoosier Boys!

By Richmond's fields, baptized with blood,
    Hoosier Boys! our Hoosier Boys!
By precious dust 'neath Shiloh's sod,
    Hoosier Boys! our Hoosier Boys!
By every martyred hero's grave,
By sacred rights they died to save,
We'll cherish in our hearts the brave
    Hoosier Boys! our Hoosier Boys!

While yet a vacant place is here,
    Hoosier Boys! our Hoosier Boys!
From hearts and homes will rise the prayer,
    Hoosier Boys! our Hoosier Boys!
"God bless our gallant men and true,
And let foul Treason meet its due!"
That faithful hearts may welcome you
    Home again, our Hoosier Boys!

WALNUT HILLS, Ohio.   MARY.

THE UNION NOW AND FOREVER.

SONG OF THE "FIGHTING BRIGADE," N. J. VOLUNTEERS.

THE Union now and forever,
  Our motto and pride shall be!
No traitor on earth shall sever
  'This glorious land of the free.
      This glorious land of the free,
      This glorious land of the free,
      No traitor on earth shall sever,
      This glorious land of the free.

The Union, now and forever,
  We 'll rally around to save!
In the face of danger ever
  The Stars and Stripes shall wave.
      The Stars and Stripes, &c.

The Union now and forever!
  We 'll bravely do or die,
And we 'll never! never! never!
  From foe or danger fly.
      From foe or danger, &c.

The Union now and forever!
  The land of liberty ;

From the foes of Freedom ever
It must and shall be free.

It must and shall be free,
It must and shall be free;
From the foes of Freedom ever
It must and shall be free.

———◆———

HOW ARE YOU, GENERAL LEE ?

OF General Lee, the Rebel chief, you all perhaps
do know
How he came North a short time since to spend a
month or so ;
But soon he found the climate warm, although a
Southern man,
And quickly hurried up his cakes, and toddled
home again.
Chorus — How are you, General Lee ? it is ; why
don't you longer stay ?
How are your friends in Maryland and
Pennsylvania ?

Jeff. Davis met him coming back ; " Why, General
Lee," he said,
" What makes you look and stagger so ? there's
whiskey in your head."

"Not much, I think," says General Lee, "No whis-
    key 's there, indeed ;
What makes me feel so giddy is, I 've taken too
    much Meade ! "
Chorus — How are you, General ? &c.

"But you seem ill, yourself, dear Jeff. You look
    quite sad enough ;
I think, while I 've been gone, Old Abe has used
    you rather rough."
"Well, yes, he has, and that 's a fact ; it makes me
    feel downcast,
For they 've bothered us at Vicksburg, so 't is
    Granted them at last. ".
Chorus — Then, how are you, Jeff. Davis ? What
    is it makes you sigh ?
       How are your friends at Vicksburg and
       in Mississippi—i ?

"Yes, Vicksburg they have got quite sure, and
    Richmond soon they 'll take ;
At Port Hudson, too, they have some Banks I fear
    we cannot break :
While Rosecrans, in Tennessee, swears he 'll our
    army flog,
And prove if Bragg 's a terrier good, Holdfast 's a
    better dog. "

Chorus — How are you, Jeff. Davis? Would you
    not like to be
        A long way out of Richmond and the
            Confederacy?
        For with " Porter " on the river, and
            " Meade " upon the land,
        I guess you 'll find that these mixed
            drinks are more than you can stand.

JUST BEFORE THE BATTLE, MOTHER.

JUST before the battle, mother,
    I am thinking most of you;
While upon the field we 're watching,
    With the enemy in view;
Comrades brave are round me lying,
    Fill'd with thoughts of home and God,
For well they know that on the morrow,
    Some will sleep beneath the sod.
Chorus —Farewell, mother, you may never
        Press me to your heart again;
        O, you 'll not forget me, mother,
            If I 'm numbered with the slain.

Oh! I long to see you, mother,
　And the loving ones at home;
But I 'll never leave our banner
　Till in honor I can come.
Tell the traitors all around you,
　That their cruel words we know,
In every battle kill our soldiers,
　By the help they give the foe.
　Farewell, mother, you may never, &c.

Hark! I hear the bugles sounding,
　'T is the signal for the fight;
Now may God protect us, mother,
　As he ever does the Right;
Hear the " Battle-Cry of Freedom,"
　How it swells upon the air —
Oh, yes, we 'll rally round the standard,
　Or we 'll perish nobly there!
　Farewell, mother, you may never, &c.

THE TRUMPET-CALL.

OVER the land the loud trumpet is calling,
　" Arm for the fight!

See ! on the battle-field thousands are falling, —
    Arm for the Right ! "

Who can delay in an hour such as this,
    Falter and stay ?
He, who his share in the nation's work miss,
    Shall rue it for aye !

Sooner or later, to us who are mortal
    Death surely will come ;
Only once in a century opens a portal
    Like this to the tomb.

You, who so selfishly shrink from the giving,
    Weakly to save,
May see whatever makes life worth the living
    Laid in the grave.

Friendship's warm hand-clasp, love's sweet caress-
      ing,
    May leave you in scorn ;
Your own heart's approval, a man's greatest bless-
      ing,
    Forever be gone.

How will you see those brave heroes returning
    Home to their land ?

Will not foul shame, on your craven cheek burning,
  Your cowardice brand ?

Hark to the Past ! its heroes are saying
  " We, too, have died ! "
Hark to the Future ! its dim voices praying —
  " For us you decide ! "

Strike on the iron, while yet it is glowing —
  Let the blow fall !
Finish the labor beyond all undoing,
  Once, and for all !

Yet there is time, O why will you lose it,
  And lingering stay ?
Your place still is waiting, O say, will you use it,
  Or cast it away ?

Hark ! the loud trumpet, its clear note repeating,
  Waits for reply ;
Says not *your heart*, keeping time with its beating,
  " *Lo ! Here am I !* "

CALAIS, Me., *Feb.* 1864.   L.

THE PATRIOT'S HYMN.

BY REV. J. F. MINES.

Air — "*America.*"

WHILE the loud drum and fife
Angrily call to strife,
    Still let us pray,
Pray God that wars may cease,
Pray God to give us peace,
Pray God our hearts release
    From discord's sway.

Yet if the sword must be
Guardian of Liberty,
    Unsheathe its blade !
Grasping the trusty brand,
Heart joined to heart, we 'll stand,
One firm, united band,
    God giving aid.

Shame to the coward come,
Death be the traitor's doom,
    Perish his name !
True be their hearts who rear
Our starry flag in air —

Ever their praise we 'll bear, —
    Deathless their fame !

Run up the Stripes and Stars,
Borne in our fathers' wars,
    Victor through all ;
For it, on battle-field,
Their sons the sword will wield !
Never that flag will yield,
    Though we may fall !

www.ingramcontent.com/pod-product-compliance
Lightning Source LLC
Chambersburg PA
CBHW021122270326
41929CB00009B/1006